D1566937

The Philosophy of Marx

Philosophy editor

Professor S. Körner
jur.Dr., Ph.D., F.B.A.
Professor of Philosophy
University of Bristol
and Yale University

The Philosophy of Marx

William Leon McBride
Professor of Philosophy,
Purdue University

St. Martin's Press   New York

For information, write:
St. Martin's Press, Inc.
175 Fifth Avenue
New York, N.Y. 10010

Printed in Great Britain
Library of Congress Catalog Card Number: 77–74774
ISBN: 0–312–60675–3
First published in the United States of America in 1977

Contents

Introduction   7

1 Aims and Subject-matters   11

2 Philosophical Influences   21

3 Marx's Method   49

4 Descriptive Generalization I:
  Materialist Metaphysics   70

5 Descriptive Generalization II:
  History and Society   92

6 Descriptive Generalization III:
  Prediction   116

7 Vision of a Possible Future   127

8 Other Marxisms   141

Conclusion   164

Select Bibliography   167

Index   171

To Angela

Introduction

The present book deals with Marx as a philosopher, rather than, primarily, as an economist, an historian, a journalist, or what have you. It is clear that Marx had the qualifications to be treated as a philosopher: it was in the field of philosophy that he earned his Doctorate, and his dissertation was adequate by the standards of the German universities of his student days. Moreover, he had a temperament that naturally revelled in extended and complex inquiry.

However, the practice of treating Marx as a philosopher may be challenged from two perspectives: from that of mainstream philosophy as it has been understood and taught in the universities in recent times, and from that of orthodox Marxism as it has come to be regarded by many of those who today label themselves Marxists. Mainstream philosophy, in both its Anglo-American and its Continental forms, has always managed to find common ground in an epistemological, metaphysical, and ethical tradition in which Hume and Kant are treated as two especially bright luminaries; Marx devoted very little space in his voluminous writings to answering the kinds of question which that tradition has considered most important. Historically speaking, Marxist orthodoxy has been identified with such names as Lenin, Castro, and Mao Tse-tung, to whom academic philosophy as a way of life seems to have been alien.

To the first objection, it may be answered that Marx does indeed have much to say about traditional philosophical questions—as, it is to be hoped, the coming pages will demonstrate—and that part of what he has to say is to provide good reasons for radically reformulating earlier conceptions of what principal tasks philosophically minded persons ought to regard as theirs. Other modern thinkers have made claims that are formally similar to this one: the names of Wittgenstein and Husserl spring to mind, for instance. To a Marxist, Marx's reformulations are simply more radical, and his reasons more cogent. Whether the new set of tasks ought still to

be called 'philosophizing' or not then turns into a merely termino-
logical question, or at best, in the universities, an administrative
one. At any rate, interest in Marx among professional teachers
and students of philosophy strikes one as being greater now than
at any time in the recent past.

The objection from the side of certain Marxist activists is epitomized in the citation from Marx's *Theses on Feuerbach* that was
selected in the 1950s as the epitaph for his Highgate Cemetery
tombstone: 'The philosophers have only interpreted the world in
various ways; the point, however, is to change it.' To conclude from
this that those who in the future stick to 'the point' must therefore
abjure philosophy depends on the assumption that 'philosophy' is a
kind of eternal essence, condemned to be the same now and in the
future as it was before Marx's time—an assumption that Marxist
philosophy strongly repudiates. There is, in fact, no compelling
reason for identifying 'philosophy' with the activities of the historical
philosophers whom Marx may have had in mind. The political
practices of many so-called orthodox Marxist movements since
Marx's death—a rich topic which we cannot hope to pursue here—
have often been seriously impoverished by the tendency to treat dis-
dainfully the movement's philosophic roots.

There does, in fact, exist a more solid basis than these for feeling
some alarm at the proposal to treat Marx as a philosopher. It lies
in the implication that we shall be engaging in a process of cutting
off just one segment, the philosophical segment, of Marx's thought
in order to scrutinize it closely. But, it will be argued, the Marxism
of Marx cannot be segmented in this way without drastically altering the character of each part and of the whole. Marxism is, as a
well-worn phrase would have it, a theory of *totality*, so that Marx
the historian is incomprehensible without Marx the economist,
Marx the economist without Marx the philosopher, and so on.
Precisely so; I agree. But what, if not philosophy, is the enterprise
of delineating this totality and indicating, through a process of
critical reflection, the relationships of major parts to major parts and
of parts to whole? (The more radical but unsustainable objection
that the mature Marx was not a philosopher at all will be answered
in detail in Chapter 1.)

It is in the spirit of attempting at once to mark off the major lines
of Marxist theory and to examine critically, often with approval and
sometimes with disapproval, Marx's reasons for placing the lines
where he did that the present account of Marx's philosophy is being

undertaken. Since the emphasis will lie in matters of philosophical interest as I have just defined these, I shall no doubt omit to consider some facets of Marx's thought that followers have considered important. But probably few major facets will be totally ignored, for Marx had the knack of uncovering philosophical issues in fields (such as economics and history) in which few other philosophers of note have thought to explore for them.

1　Aims and Subject-matters

It is not quite correct to claim, as do some teachers of philosophy, that a philosopher's thought can adequately be understood in complete independence of his subjective intentions, or the purposes that he had in mind in writing what he did. At the very least, the philosopher's own conception of his ultimate aims is certain to influence his choice of the subject-matters to which he devotes attention, and the ways in which he approaches them. Moreover, the idea that there can be *purely* 'subjective' intentions, uninfluenced by objectively verifiable events in the thinker's life, is an illusion. Marx began his career at a time when a climate of idealism, in which such an illusion is able to flourish, was still dominant in his native Germany, and throughout his lifetime he combated this, laying the greatest stress on the inescapable role of objective, socio-economic realities in moulding the ideas in individuals' heads, even when the individuals themselves are oblivious of it.

Thus it makes sense to begin by inquiring both what it was that Marx thought he was doing by way of a career, and what, in retrospect, he can be seen actually to have done. In fact, these questions are more important in his case than in that of most philosophers, precisely because the break that he intended to effect with 'the philosophers', the mere world-interpreters, of the past was to be so sharp. Western philosophy, in its twenty-five-century history, exhibits many continuities, including those of two general, complementary traditions: dogmatic assertion about the nature of reality ('system-building') and scepticism about knowledge-claims. Even today would-be philosophers are trained to learn appropriate moves —some of the questions to ask, some of the potential naïveties to avoid—from a study of the history of these two traditions, and thus to make themselves feel more at home in the inherently odd role of philosopher by imitating prominent role-models from one or both of them. There is a large element of both traditions in the thought of Marx—his materialist theory of society and history on the one side, his critique of ideological thinking on the other—and we shall of course be examining subsequently some of his inheritances from past schools of thought. But there was also something more in him, which made him uncomfortable with the very role of philosopher, conceived of as someone who confines himself to elaborating new, presumably more satisfactory, answers to the old questions of who we are and what we can know. The additional element is Marx's driving commitment actively to change 'the world', whatever that might turn out to mean in his thought, and that is why a preliminary inquiry into his career aims is so particularly necessary.

It is not the case that Marx was always thoroughly clear concerning his intentions. He began his university life with certain poetic and other literary ambitions in mind, and he went through a brief epoch of law studies, largely under paternal pressure. He then turned to philosophy, in which he completed his Doctoral research and writing, and at this time he entertained some hope of obtaining an academic post. Although nascent strands of his later thought can be detected in his writings of this early period, his theoretical orientation was still nearly as ambiguous and indefinite as were his career plans.

It would be a mistake to think of *either* ambiguity as having been thoroughly dissipated by the time of Marx's death. On the career side, this is easy to document. Marx was, as much as any nineteenth-century European and more than most, the plaything of the century's major historical currents. Unable to teach or even to remain intellectually active in the politically repressive Prussia of the early 1840s, prohibited from continuing his brief career as editor of a progressive newspaper in Cologne, he moved first to Paris and shortly thereafter, the victim of an expulsion order by the French Interior Ministry, to Brussels. Within the next few years, against the background of the Europe-wide revolutionary ferment before and during 1848 and of its aftermath, he found himself at different times acquiring some reputation as an author, applying for papers to emigrate to America, negotiating in London with the newly formed Communist League to draw up his famous *Manifesto*, welcomed back to Paris during the short-lived Republican regime, engaging in political and journalistic activity (and even in a fund-raising tour for his newspaper) back in Germany and ultimately settling in London, his home for the remainder of his life. Marx was by no means convinced, at the time of his move to London, either that it would be his permanent residence or that research, and writing the material that we know in its final form as *Capital*, would be his predominant lifetime activity. He regarded himself, especially during the early London years, as an exile, awaiting the upheaval that would make it possible for him to re-establish himself safely and permanently in his homeland; even in later years, he and his family often discussed the possibility of returning. Although he did come to consider himself as primarily a serious theoretical writer by profession, at least during the putatively interim period of reactionary political dominance in Germany, his financial difficulties were notorious, and so he once even applied to be a railway clerk (but was refused because of his illegible handwriting). He also spent much time, particularly in the 1870s, in political organizing, and it was his journalistic contributions to the New York *Tribune*, particularly in the late 1850s, and to other newspapers that helped keep him from total financial ruin at crucial moments.

One might argue that, given the highly non-esoteric character of Marx's philosophical thought, even his newspaper articles and many of his contributions to political groups (e.g., his *The Civil War in France*, which was first delivered as an address to the General Council of the International Working-men's Association, or his *Critique of the Gotha Programme* of the German Social Democratic Party, which was a private communication, first published years after his death) must be considered as integral parts of his total theoretical work. This claim has much to recommend it, but it raises further questions concerning just how Marx's overall theoretical programme is to be conceived. As a writer, Marx devoted an inordinate amount of time to matters that in retrospect appear to have been peripheral to his own principal aims. Oddly enough, some of the polemical writings that he succeeded in getting into print prior to the publication of Volume I of *Capital*—most notably, *The Holy Family* and *Herr Vogt*, the latter an acrimonious attack on an obscure figure that occupied Marx's attention for more than a year during the midst of his work on *Capital*—now appear, by general consensus, to be of less importance for understanding Marxism than are some of the numerous manuscripts that he willingly left unpublished. Although more than fifteen years elapsed between the completion of Volume I of *Capital* and Marx's death, it was left to Friedrich Engels, Marx's lifelong collaborator, to complete the preparation of Volumes II and III for posthumous publication; Volume III, in particular, which resolves several fundamental questions about Marx's economic theory that Volume I leaves unanswered, was still in quite chaotic shape when it fell to Engels to edit it. This anomalous situation is explicable in part by Marx's poor physical condition in his later years, in part by the numerous divergent demands that were made on his time, and in part by certain psychological traits—e.g., a combination of scholarly perfectionism and somewhat inefficient work habits—that are traceable throughout his adult years. But all such explanations remain inadequate, and we need to probe further.

Marx was profoundly convinced both of the correctness of his philosophy (of course) and of the imminent inevitability of a Europewide upheaval of some sort, beginning in any one of several countries, that would ultimately bring to political power forces sympathetic to the working class. (A more precise formulation of his expectations for the immediate future would probably be misleading.) To Marx's mind, these two convictions no doubt appeared to be more or less of a piece, at least in the sense that they implied no serious conflict. From our distance, however, we may be excused for seeing it differently. From a theoretical point of view, as I shall show in Chapter 6, there is nothing in Marx's analysis of his own society and of its historical tendencies that would force or even *enable* a reader of *Capital*, at the time of its publication in the autumn of 1867, to conclude that an upheaval of the general sort that Marx personally anticipated would be certain to take place within any specifiable future time-period. Practically speaking, many of the incompletenesses and irregularities of Marx's theoretical productivity are attributable to the disharmony between his philosophic convictions and his confidence in the imminence of upheaval.

There were occasions on which Marx half feared, half hoped, that he would be forced to break off his theoretical activity—itself always being expanded as new data and relevant new literature were brought to his attention—in order to participate in the organization of a post-revolutionary order in one or another place. At the same time, the scope of his theoretical vision and consequently of his ambitions as a philosopher was truly global. (In a man of Marx's degree of intellectual seriousness, his commitment to the old dictum, '*Nihil humanum a me alienum puto*' [I regard nothing human as foreign to me], should be thought of as expressing a fairly literal self-image, rather than a stylized conceit.) Moreover, to Marx, global generalizations in the absence of vast arrays of supportive detail were worthless—as the enormous length of *Capital* and many of his other writings attests. We may conclude that the intellectual projects of a thinker of Marx's sort could not possibly be realized in the space of a lifetime, even if he had not undergone the distractions occasioned by his excessively optimistic expectations concerning the course of current events. Given such expectations, it should be no surprise that Marx actually completed far less as a theorist than he had intended in mid-career.

This is important, because it permits us from the outset to attack a common interpretation of Marx's theoretical development that has consequences for understanding his ultimate aims. The interpretation runs something like this: a content analysis of what Marx wrote after the 1840s simply illustrates a decision that he had reached to quit philosophy and to become a professional economic theorist; Marx made this decision, it is then alleged, because he had arrived at the belief that economic factors were the sole causal determinants of both history and thought.

This interpretation finds support in certain ambiguous passages in the short Preface to Marx's *A Contribution to the Critique of Political Economy*, one of the few texts in which he attempts to describe his own career. When Marx speaks there of having had to 'settle accounts with [his] former philosophical conscience' (by writing his and Engels's posthumously published *The German Ideology*) and of turning thenceforth to the study of political economy, it is easy to conclude from this the existence of a radical break in his development. But Marx himself (even if we set aside his many references elsewhere to intended projects in areas other than the strictly economic, and focus on what he has to say in this one text, in which he is attempting to present his credentials as an economist to the reading public) appears to treat the evolution of his theoretical interests at that early time, including his rejection of the idealist presuppositions of German philosophy, as something less than a conversion-experience. Rather, the development appears to have consisted in a growth of clarity concerning the anti-idealist principles that were to guide his future research. These heuristic principles—namely, that one must look to 'the material conditions of life' to explain the structure of society, and that political economy provides the best clues for understanding the nature of these material conditions—do not amount to the dogmatic, *a priori* claim of total economic determinism into which they were later erected by some of Marx's followers. Moreover, the argument used to support them could only be given, as Marx was aware, from a point of view external to the science of political economy itself.

We can better grasp this, in the interest of further clarifying Marx's basic aims, by considering his reasons for employing the word 'critique' to characterize his major endeavour. ('A Critical Analysis of Capitalist Production' is the sub-title of *Capital*.) The word was much in vogue among nineteenth-century German intellectuals; the major historical source of this vogue had been Immanuel Kant. Kant's aim, in his *Critique of Pure Reason*, had been to undermine the pretensions of reason on its theoretical side, by rigorously demonstrating its incapacity to reach certitude about the ultimate truths that, in the mainstream of Western philosophy, it had traditionally been thought capable of attaining. Political economy had arisen as a recognizable science during Kant's own lifetime (Kant and Adam Smith were contemporaries), and had itself appeared to exhibit an exemplary rigour of a novel sort— 'the interesting spectacle [. . .] of thought working upon the endless mass of details [. . .] and extracting therefrom the simple principles of the thing', in Hegel's sarcastically intended words. Marx became convinced early on, during the years immediately following his Doctoral work, both that the kinds of item (wealth, exchange transactions, productive labour, etc.) upon which the political economists concentrated their attention could, correctly comprehended, provide the basis for satisfactorily explaining major aspects of the world in which we live (as the spiritual entities of Hegelian and neo-Hegelian philosophy could not), and yet that sarcasm concerning the ultimate truth-claims of the classical political economists was justified. Specifically, Marx detected a kind of absolutism in the thought of Smith and his successors, according to which the general rules and practices of the economic system—the capitalist market system—as they had analysed it were assumed to be irreplaceable, historically speaking, by any radically new set of rules and practices—barring a regression to some primitive economic form. Marx's 'critiquing' of political economy, then, had the dual purpose of showing that this absolutist assumption on the part of the political economists was invalid and that the actual system contained tendencies that were at once potentially destructive of the existing system itself and potentially generative of a new, non-primitive system.

Now, let us call this envisaged new system of rules and practices a 'society of associated producers', as Marx himself did in his occasional references to it in *Capital*; we thus avoid some of the misleading historical baggage with which the words 'communism' and 'socialism' are laden. One salient characteristic of it by contrast with present-day society, in Marx's view, would be that in it what we call economic factors would play a considerably smaller role in people's lives than they do today. Consequently, the exclusive determination of history and thought by economic factors (assuming that the word 'economic' is being used in something like the ordinary sense) does not obtain at least in Marx's vision of a possible future, post-capitalist society. (In fact, as we shall see in Chapter 5, it cannot obtain in Marx's description of the present and past, either.)

The paradoxicality of Marx's theoretical aims and of the 'critical standpoint' from which he undertook to accomplish them should by now begin to become evident—more evident than it often seemed to Marx himself, to judge from his occasional self-descriptions, and more evident than it ever seemed to his intelligent, devoted, but overly facile collaborator and popularizer, Engels. Just as Kant's success in undermining the claims of reason through rational inquiry raises perplexing questions about the point of view from which he himself could possibly be writing, so one is moved to raise equally hard questions concerning Marx's perspective as he undermines the science of political economy from within. At any rate, it cannot be that of an economist, pure and simple.

There is an easy, slogan-like answer available to the question of what Marx's own standpoint is: it is the standpoint of the proletariat. But what is the standpoint of the proletariat, or rather what was it during Marx's lifetime? It can certainly not be equated with some non-existent, imagined empirical consensus of the social views and aspirations of all propertyless, subsistence-salaried industrial workers (the group that most clearly counts as 'the proletariat' in Marxian usage) at a given time in the nineteenth century. Marx was always acutely aware of the deep rifts that existed within the workers' movements of his day. The ambiguity involved in designating Marxism's standpoint as that of the proletariat cannot satisfactorily be eliminated, as Lenin and others later attempted to do, by identifying the interests of the proletariat with the goals formulated by its 'vanguard' Party, for this simply raises new questions about the validity of the Party's claims.

Let us try now to resolve the issues of Marx's theoretical standpoint, and hence of the paradox that his theoretical aims were not those of the professional economist, even though the subject-matter of economics occupied so much of his attention. As a result of empirical observation and reflection, Marx accepted and promulgated the view of society as consisting of hostile classes having conflicting fundamental interests. In his day he took the conflict between two principal classes, the owners of capital and those who worked for them, to be most significant, and in ongoing manifestations of that conflict he sided with the workers whenever the issues appeared sufficiently clear-cut to him. He regarded this practical activity as harmonious with, and biographically speaking the outcome of, his theoretical outlook. But the actual industrial proletariat—and hence the notion of a 'proletarian standpoint'—takes on its full *meaning* for Marx, beyond the available statistics about numbers of factory workers and their salaries in the mid-nineteenth century, only within the context of a general theory (or, if 'theory' sounds too speculative and detached from other life activities, world-view). How is this the case?

In the Hegelian language of which Marx was fonder in his early years, the proletariat was said to have the function of a 'universal class'. In Hegel's political philosophy that role had been assigned to the class of government bureaucrats, since they at once participated, by working to earn their livelihoods, in the business life of the community, the sphere of the capitalist market economy that Hegel designated as 'civil society', and at the same time contributed, by virtue of the *kind* of work that they did, to the supposedly higher, reconciling, and harmonizing set of activities in modern society that Hegel denominated 'the State'. Marx considered the view of the modern State as a higher, quasi-divine reality to be dangerous nonsense, and his attitude towards bureaucracy was one of contempt. But he did take seriously the notion that a single social class, distinguishable from the other classes by differences in sets of interests and specifically in its relationship to property, could be at least potentially 'universal'. That is, the proletariat, which as defined by Marx (propertyless and subsistence-salaried) held no part of the riches of modern society and thus had 'nothing to lose', could, if and when it abolished the existing power relationships within which it occupied a position of extreme subordination, put an end to private ownership of the means of production and to class divisions as such, and hence to the clash of irreconcilable basic interests associated with these phenomena. (In the pithy words of the *Internationale*, '*Nous ne sommes rien; soyons tout*' [We have been nothing; we shall be all.] This is, essentially, the meaning of the famous Marxian notion of a 'classless society'; it provides us with a *leitmotif* to explain at once Marx's active commitment to the advancement of workers' movements and his fundamental motivations for engaging in the kind of scholarly theorizing in political economy that occupied most of his later career.

The two kinds of activities really were, to Marx's way of thinking, identical in ultimate aim. This is the meaning, in Marx's career, of the fabled, mystical-sounding 'unity of theory and practice'. The fact that he conceived of his life's work in this fashion does indeed distinguish him, in all probability, from most other major figures in the history of Western philosophy. Be this as it may, we are now in a position to understand why the Marxism of Marx is not primarily an economic theory—that is, why the role of strictly economic factors within the overall Marxian philosophy is dispro-portionately smaller than the amount of time and effort that Marx himself devoted to economic research.

Marx was most interested in theories of society, social philo-sophies—not so much for their own sakes, but for the light that they might shed on the possibility of changing the quality of day-to-day social life. From his own direct experience, apart from all theorizing, he found social life in the western Europe of his day to be radically unsatisfactory—riven by extreme inequalities in wealth, and hence in the capacities of individuals to meet their own needs, material and intellectual; in the growing class of industrial prole-tarians he found the most extreme victims of this state of affairs. This experience, in combination with the accidents of his educational background and evolution, led him to produce, across several decades and through the career uncertainties and intellectual am-biguities that I have described and many more, the body of thought that is known as Marxism. Marx's decision to concentrate, in his later career, on economic phenomena in elaborating his theory reflects his intellectual conviction that along that path lay the road to greater explanatory power concerning society in his day than along any other. But this did not and could not, rationally speaking, entail a prior dogmatic claim on his part that only economic factors mattered for the ultimate understanding of society, and hence that Marxism was primarily a new theory in economics. Rather, he is inviting us to look hard at economic determinations of society, for therein, he is convinced and is prepared to argue, lies the best path to enlightenment. But this invitation, like his concomitant commit-ment to the standpoint of the proletariat, needs to be understood within a wider philosophical context.

It is with this need in mind that I have planned the remainder of the present book. In Chapter 2 I shall discuss some of the leading *philosophical* influences on Marx's thought. The next five chapters will be organized in accordance with my belief, which I hope will prove to be comparatively uncontroversial, that a theory of as global a scope as Marx's can be divided into three interconnected but logically distinguishable components: its methodology, its descriptions of the world (or of parts thereof), and its 'normative' or ideal element. Marx's method and his 'vision of a possible future', as I prefer to call the normative element in his thought, will occupy Chapters 3 and 7 respectively, while the descriptive component will in turn be divided into three segments—Marxism as an ontology or set of generalizations about reality as a whole, Marx's interpretative account of past and contemporary history and society, and Marxism as a purported set of predictions about the future—and treated in the corresponding Chapters 4, 5 and 6. Finally, in Chapter 8, I shall survey and evaluate some of the principal twentieth-century philosophical developments that claim Marx as their inspiration, but that diverge significantly and interestingly from him in philosophical style and in the subject-matters that they stress, if not in conceptual thrust.

In attempting to clarify Marx's basic theoretical aims in the present chapter, I have of course made use of textual evidence to engage in a certain amount of systematic reconstruction. This is inevitable; the legacy of Marx's written works is vast and disparate. But I have been both faithful and generally sympathetic to his ideas, while raising occasional criticisms about unresolved ambiguities. This will be my approach throughout. The philosophical spirit, which was characteristic of Marx to a very high degree, is essentially a critical one, apt at detecting disappointing inconsistencies and gaps in the thought of others, far less gifted in constructing the virtually impregnable new thought-edifices at which, in principle, it aims. If the final verdict concerning Marx's philosophy is that it too falls under this description, then so be it. Nevertheless, the far-reaching quality of its aims and the cogency of some of the chains of reasoning that are integral to it make it uniquely valuable among the social theories of the modern age.

2 Philosophical Influences

Engels maintained that Marxian socialism was the product of three principal intellectual traditions, plus the novel insights of Marx's own creative genius. (Most notable in the latter category, in Engels's opinion, were the materialist theory of history and the view that the creation of surplus value by human labour-power is the clue to the accumulation of capital in the capitalist system.) The three traditions were those of bourgeois political economy, of socialism (the previous major proponents of which Engels labelled 'utopians'), and of dialectical philosophy, culminating in Hegel. In this chapter we shall be concerned with the last of these strands.

To the dialectical tradition, Engels opposed what he called the 'narrow, metaphysical mode of thinking'; this terminology itself goes back to Hegel. Curiously, those whom Engels and Hegel primarily intended by the pejorative epithet 'metaphysicians' are the empiricist ancestors, such as Locke, of the groups of analytical thinkers who are today most likely to regard Hegel and other Continentals as 'metaphysicians' in a destructive, obscurantist sense. What has remained constant is the pejorative emotive connotation. It is true that Marx always warned against an excessively analytic outlook, especially in the sense of a failure to perceive relationships among the parts of a total social structure. But it is rather difficult to specify more exactly just what unites all the figures in the history of philosophy with whom Marx claimed a particular affinity. Engels traces the origin of dialectical thought to Heraclitus, the pre-Socratic Greek whose surviving fragments of fascinating but Delphic utterances convince us that his traditional label, 'the Obscure', was well earned. Stylistically speaking, at least, it would be difficult to find a figure more remote from Marx.

Instead of attempting to discover a unilinear development in pre-Marxian thought that may not in fact exist in any very plausible sense, I shall discuss what I consider to be Marx's most important philosophical inheritances under three general headings: the Greeks,

Hegel, and Marx's contemporaries. Although Marx admired and presumably learned something from other philosophers, such as Leibniz, and although he also learned lessons, albeit primarily of a negative sort, from such frequent objects of his attacks as Locke, Berkeley, and Hume, these influences seem to be weaker than those that I have selected. The Greeks were the objects of Marx's earliest intensive study, and references to Aristotle occur at crucial points in his later writings. There are Hegel-lovers and Hegel-haters among Marxists and Marxologists, but it is unthinkable that any serious modern student of Marx would dismiss Hegel as insignificant for Marx's development. And finally, the atmosphere of Young Hegelianism that the young Marx breathed, and of which he was at one time a part, his rejection of Feuerbach, and his intellectual relationship with Engels are all of obviously great importance in understanding his philosophy.

(a) The Greeks

Marx participated actively in the enthusiasm for Greek civilization that was general among German intellectuals in his youth. His dissertation concerned the difference between the Democritean and Epicurean philosophies of nature. His choice of two dissenters from the theistically and metaphysically oriented mainstream of Greek philosophy (at least as that mainstream has been defined by the Christian West) is interesting, although it is also the case that these two thinkers, whose literary remains are so fragmentary, pose less formidable a challenge for a dissertation than does Plato or Aristotle. Of somewhat more significance than the choice of topics itself is Marx's expressed preference for the philosophy of Epicurus over that of Democritus: it is based on Marx's belief that the former's conception of basic particles ('atoms') is more satisfactory than the latter's in accounting for the existence of freedom and energy in the world. (Epicurus had maintained the doctrine that an infinitesimal 'swerve' occurred in the movement of some of the atoms through space; this 'swerve' was the source of free action; thus, total prior determinism was rendered impossible.) It is not, I think, far-fetched to see in this choice an anticipation of the crucial distinction that he was to draw, a few years later, between his 'naturalism', with its emphasis on the peculiar, active quality of human *praxis*, and the excessive mechanism of his fellow-materialists of the eighteenth century.

Some of the notes that Marx took while preparing to write his dissertation have survived. They show the breadth of his readings in and about Greek philosophy, as well as a strong tendency on his part to draw an historical parallel between his own era and the period following Aristotle's death. Hegel had been the modern Aristotle, in the young Marx's eyes. The notes display great ambivalence concerning the age in which Marx was living, with a tone of romantic pessimism dominant. It was clear to Marx that philosophy was forced to take a drastically new tack, now that a system as total as Hegel's had just been elaborated, but he showed considerable uncertainty as to what the historical precedents of Stoicism, Scepticism, and Epicureanism, the post-Aristotelean philosophies, with their predominant stress on ethical conduct and inwardness in a universe seen as governed by fate, betokened for the philosophy of the immediate future.

What remained of all this in Marx's developed thought was his interest in the Greek world (as exemplified in his uncharacteristic attribution to Greek art of an eternal value, or at least of some qualities that permit of a renewal of esteem in different historical forms of society) and his high admiration for Aristotle. He had taken notes on Plato as well, and certain features of the latter's *Republic*, especially its class divisions, continued to command his attention at various points in his later writings. But it was Aristotle who, for Marx as for Hegel, best epitomized the brilliance of ancient Greek society and its cultural limitations.

Slavery was the economic base upon which Greek society maintained its comparatively high living standard. Aristotle is well known for his ethical defence of slavery, on the ground that there are some biologically human beings whose low natural aptitudes are such as to be fully realizable only if they act as the mere instruments, or tools, of others. Since for Aristotle what is best is what conforms as closely as possible with this normative conception of nature and the natural, it follows that those who are slaves by nature ought actually to function as slaves. He admits that such contingencies as the spoils of warfare sometimes result in the actual enslavement of the wrong people—i.e., some who are not natural slaves. But the important thing, for the philosopher, is the validity of the principle.

Marx wastes no time in venting fashionable moral outrage against an argument that, to the typical modern mind (though not to the American slaveholder, Marx's contemporary, prior to the war between the states), seems nothing more than a self-serving rationalization. Rather he sees in Aristotle's chain of reasoning an example, excellent by virtue of its familiarity and of the unquestioned acumen of its author, of ideological thinking, the usually unselfconscious employment of supposedly disinterested theorists in justifying the institutional arrangements of dominance and subordination that characterize the particular historical forms of society in which they live. The Aristotelean defence of slavery was rooted in the plausible principle, central to Aristotle's entire system of thought, of the desirability of maximally realizing the inherent potentialities of every entity. That the potentialities of large numbers of humanoid creatures, the 'natural slaves', were severely limited was an apparent fact of which Aristotle received abundant confirmation in his social experience. He ultimately could not, despite his genius, see beyond the limitations of his social group's assumptions.

There is, however, at least one passage in Aristotle's *Politics* in which he seems momentarily to do so, and it is of significance for understanding Marx's point of view in *Capital*. In it Aristotle alludes to the possibility of a world, to him wholly imaginary, in which what we call automated machinery could take the places of slaves and apprentices. In such a world, he points out (by way of underscoring the reasonableness of hierarchical relationships in the world as it really is), there would be no need for the distinctions of master and slave or of master craftsman and apprentice. Marx, after paying tribute to Aristotle as 'the greatest thinker of antiquity', comments with heavy irony on the passage in question: the Greeks, he says, 'understood nothing of Political Economy and Christianity', which have shown the way to using modern machinery for the purpose of prolonging the working day and perpetuating a new kind of slavery. Marx is always rather precise in insisting on distinctions: wageslavery is a *new* kind of slavery, not at all the *same* as either ancient slavery or feudal serfdom. But the two sorts of subordination between classes of human beings do have some important features in common; exploitation and a form (total in the one case, partial in the other) of possession of man by man characterize both.

If one were to try to name the single concept that is most important of all in Aristotle's philosophy, 'nature' would seem to be the most obvious choice. The historical significance of this fact for later Western thought and even language is impossible to exaggerate. Various schools of 'natural law' dominated medieval thinking about ethics and politics, and early modern political theorists such as Hobbes and Locke all took it for granted that in some sense or other, the diverse senses often being quite disparate and incompatible, human conduct ought ideally to be regulated in accordance with what was most natural. Later, the idea of natural laws and propensities was employed in an ostensibly more descriptive than normative sense in the burgeoning natural and social sciences, including political economy. Whereas in Aristotle the factual and normative uses of the term 'nature' had come ultimately to the same thing, since to act in accordance with nature was to realize fully what in fact were the entity's potentialities, modern 'scientific' references to natural laws were (and to some extent still are, even today) alleged to describe what was demonstrably the case in the area under investigation, whether or not one liked what was the case or found it to be ideal in any way. But still implicit in the designation of certain general 'laws' as 'natural' was the notion that to attempt to bring about events not in conformity with them, or to replace one set of these 'laws' with another, was unscientific, foolish, and ultimately doomed to failure. In this way, for instance, political economists frequently made use of the adjective 'natural' to characterize the rules of the capitalist market system. Thus, across a number of transformations, this Aristotelean intellectual heritage remained vital into Marx's nineteenth century.

Marx's youthful writings, particularly his *1844 Manuscripts*, are filled with references to his thought as a 'naturalism' (which he equates with 'humanism') and to the possibilities of human beings becoming fully 'natural' in a society in which present-day forms of social alienation had been abolished. In these manuscripts Marx is at once working towards a new conception of society, often couched in somewhat vague and poetical terms, and carrying on a polemic against Hegel's relegation of nature to a necessary but negative position within his idealist philosophy of 'Spirit'. A disharmony exists at present, Marx is claiming, between the social roles that all (capitalists and others as well as workers) are compelled to play, and their qualities of being parts of nature; this disharmony can be overcome at some future time, and then, he vaguely but intriguingly suggests, even the human senses would acquire new functions. Although Aristotle is rarely mentioned by name in these early Marxian speculations, recognition of his influence sheds light on Marx's efforts to eliminate idealist premises from his thinking. Above all, Aristotle was to Marx a philosopher who took sense experience as his starting-point and, by contrast with the idealists, held all that was 'natural' in high esteem. Marx, along with most of his contempor-

aries, rejected the static, unchanging character of nature as conceived by Aristotle, but he retained and even reintroduced some of
the normative functions that Aristotle had attributed to it; the
concept of *human* nature, in particular, represented a possible
future ideal, rather than an already existing reality, for the young
Marx.

In the *Theses on Feuerbach*, written in 1845, Marx attacked the
traditional notion of a fixed human essence or nature, holding that
the concept of such an essence could be used to refer validly only to
'the ensemble of social relationships' at a given time in history. In
this limited sense, he did break with certain aspects of his philosophical past, including his self-image as a philosopher of 'naturalism'; this term never again played a prominent role in his writings.
Thenceforth he felt a greater fascination for the technological ideal
of *dominating* nature (at least the non-human portion of it), of ex-
ploiting its resources for the sake of material progress. But he continued to retain a considerable amount of Aristotelean respect for
nature, and he used this concept, together with some others that were
related to it in classical thought, as an important tool of criticism.
In this usage, 'nature' and the 'natural' do not generally serve as
positive descriptive epithets, as they still did in the writings of the
bourgeois political economists, but as a conceptual reference-point
against which to contrast the limitations of existing 'conventional'
arrangements.

At the beginning of *Capital* and of other later writings, Marx
explicitly accepts the Aristotelean distinction between use-values and
exchange-values. All exchangeable goods, Aristotle maintained, are
simultaneously characterized by these two sorts of values, which are
strictly incommensurable with one another. The concept of use-value
refers to a good's direct utility in satisfying natural human needs.
Most useful goods can also be exchanged for other useful goods,
however, and it is this quality that constitutes their exchange-value.
Analysing the crude, pre-capitalist exchange system of the ancient
world, Aristotle acknowledged that exchange was a 'natural' activity, but regarded the phenomenon of exchange-value as suspicious.
With the rise of trade among cities, he saw, a medium of exchange,
money, had become necessary; this had led to what he called the
unnatural, as opposed to the natural, form of the art of acquisition,
and ultimately to the misconception that money-making was the
goal to which all other life activities should be subordinated. Of
course, Marx does not regard Aristotle's elaboration of the distinc-

tion as being at all satisfactory for present purposes, but he considers the *Politics* to contain the fundamental critical insights that he wants. The analysis of the exchange-values, rather than the use-values, of 'commodities' (the technical name for exchangeable goods in a market system) occupies virtually his entire attention throughout the remainder of *Capital*, but the distinction between the two forms of value remains crucial. This is particularly true with respect to Marx's understanding of the contrast between capitalist and post-capitalist societies.

In the former, it is clear to Marx, exchange-values dominate, in the sense that they preoccupy the attention of the actors in the system most of the time. Production of commodities takes place, not in accordance with the criteria of social needs, but in accordance with the requirement that their exchange-values (which Marx, in common with the bourgeois political economists, assumes commodities to have acquired by virtue of being the products of human labour) be maximized in relation to other commodities on the market and to investment. This gives rise to the condition that Marx calls the 'fetishism of commodities', whereby these objects *appear* to be acting in accordance with strict rules of their own, independently of the wishes of those who have produced them. (We shall return to these matters in Chapter 5.) In a conceivable post-capitalist system, by contrast, Marx maintains (in his very brief and occasional references to it) that the relative social use-values of goods would be the primary criteria in the ordering of priorities for production and distribution.

It is not just an initial technical distinction that Marx shares with Aristotle; it is a fundamental normative view of the social world. For both, the contrast between 'convention' and 'nature' and the preference for the latter are essentially the same. Marx regards the capitalist exchange system, created and maintained by mutual, if passive, consent, as distortive of nature, in the sense that what is produced by it fails to 'fit' at all well with actual human needs; he holds this while at the same time maintaining (and I see no logical inconsistency here) that these needs themselves are historically relative and that the inception of a future, need-oriented, post-capitalist society would be inconceivable without the prior historical occurrence of a capitalist epoch. In this way Marx is able drastically to relativize the claims of the political economists concerning the supreme 'naturalness' of the capitalist system, retaining something of his earlier view of an as yet unrealized but possible harmony between human institutions and nature as the standpoint from which to undertake his radical criticism.

We can observe this fundamental normative orientation with particular clarity if we consider Marx's reaction to the condemnation of usury that, like the defence of slavery and the use-value/exchange-value distinction, is to be found in Book I of Aristotle's *Politics*. In a passage that was to be of great importance for Medieval Christianity, and through it for the thought of Martin Luther (whom Marx cites approvingly on the subject) as well as for Marx, Aristotle denounced usury, meaning the charging of *any* interest on money loaned, as being against nature. He called it 'money breeding money'; it was conventionalism carried, as it were, to the second degree, since the conventional establishment of money as a medium of exchange had already represented a departure from the more 'natural' process of barter. While Aristotle saw both advantages and disadvantages in the use of money, which at any rate had obviously become a practical necessity in his day, he saw only a threat to decent social life in the practice of charging interest. The entire passage in question is cited without comment, but with implicit approval, at a point in *Capital* in which Marx is discussing money-lending as the extreme form, M—M' of the standard formula of capitalist accumulation, M—C—M' (where M stands for money, C for commodity, and the sign ' for an increment).

This discussion is of particularly great importance because of the role that Marx assigns to accumulation. The distinctive characteristic of capitalism by comparison with all other economic systems, Marx indicates at several points, is its intrinsic tendency to foster unlimited accumulation of capital (in the sense of requiring the human actors in the system to contribute to this process under penalty of personal ruin for failing to do so) for its own sake, without regard to further consequences. He claims scientifically to have solved, through his detailed economic analyses of the phenomenon that he calls 'surplus-value', the puzzle as to *how* this takes place. In arriving at this solution, he owes nothing to Aristotle or to any other ancient philosopher. But in the initial description of what it is that takes place, and in the critical stance that he takes towards it, Marx's debt is heavy indeed, and he sometimes, at crucial points, acknowledges it.

As fundamental to Aristotle's world-view as his complex and all-embracing conception of nature is the concomitant abhorrence, shared with most Greek thinkers and ordinary Greeks, that he feels for the unlimited, the 'boundless'. To Aristotle the individual or the society that yields to boundless and 'excess' insatiable acquisitive instincts is by definition depraved; the conceptual and factual connection between the two terms of the definition is so close in Aristotle's mind that it would be misleading to call this a mere 'value-judgement' on his part, as if an alternative judgement were conceivable. The same can be said of Marx's conception of capitalism as a system of unlimited accumulation. Perhaps, at a time at which the scarcity (i.e. the limitedness) of natural resources is again becoming a matter of great concern we may rediscover some specifiable meaning, as Marx did, in the Ancients' seemingly primitive horror of the boundless and in their corresponding respect for 'nature'.

It is less easy, however, to justify the other positive use that Marx made of the adjective 'natural', the use that he shared with the many nineteenth-century scientists and social scientists who wrote with confidence about the 'natural laws' that they had discovered. When Marx speaks of his having unearthed the 'natural laws of motion' of a certain form (the capitalist form) of society, as well as (at least by implication) the laws of transition from one form to the next, he is committing himself to a view, which he elsewhere repudiates, of all human history as consisting of a series of 'natural', inevitable, perhaps even predictable, developments; the modern self-image of humanity as historical thus becomes reabsorbed into a new, more complicated, but once again ultimately *static* conception of 'nature' and the 'natural'. Much of the value for criticism (particularly of the political economists) that Marx derived from the underlying normative conception of nature that I have just delineated is lost when this more recent variety of 'natural law' theory is brought to the fore, and instead a new, dogmatic metaphysics is erected. We shall have to come to grips with this latter version of Marxism at later points in this book. Here I can only point out that it too has its root origins in the fascination with Nature that Marx inherited from Aristotle, more than from any other philosopher.

(b) Hegel

No one questions the importance of Hegel in Marx's early intellectual development, but thereafter disputes abound. In the abundant literature of Marx scholarship, readers are frequently treated to exegeses of such words as 'coquetting' (Marx admitted to having 'coquetted' with Hegelian forms of expression in his later works, as a sort of reaction against the patronizing attitude towards Hegel that became voguish in Germany about the middle of the century) and of such phrases as 'discovering the rational kernel in the mystical shell' [of Hegel's thought] or 'standing Hegel's dialectic on its head—or rather, on its feet', both of which activities Marx boasted of having engaged in. These casually intended metaphors, when scrutinized very closely, can give rise to volumes of ponderings. For instance, if one coquets with another person, can one at the same time take that person seriously, or not? The answers to such questions provide fuel for the debate about Hegel's influence on Marx.

Most simply put, the debate comes to this: ought Marx to be regarded as a continuer of the Hegelian tradition, who substituted certain new premises for Hegel's while preserving basic Hegelian patterns of thought, or ought Marx's radical rejection of Hegelianism be considered one of the most important events in his intellectual development? The answer is, 'Both'. Lenin, whose early studies of Marxism had included almost no explicit elements of Hegelian philosophy, made the perceptive comment, late in his life, that Marx had not been understood by any of the Marxists of his generation, because none of them had read Hegel's *Logic*. (The remark is contained in notes, later published, that Lenin took while reading extensively in Hegel and Aristotle.) This does not necessarily imply, I take it, that those Marxists' theoretical commitments were totally at odds with Marx's own, but rather that their ignorance of the extent of Hegel's influence on Marx deprived them of a crucial element in explaining Marx's general philosophical framework.

Marx's flirtation with Hegel began during Marx's student days at Berlin. Hegel, dead a mere five years at the time of Marx's arrival, had occupied the academic chair of philosophy there, and his influence remained great both in philosophy and in the law faculty, although of course there were also detractors. In a letter to his father that has been preserved, Marx reveals that his first reaction upon reading some of Hegel's philosophy was more negative than positive, both because of its convoluted style and because of its idealism. Nevertheless, Marx joined a discussion group of students and younger instructors, the nucleus of what history has come to call 'the Young Hegelians', and spent considerable time analysing Hegel's works in detail. One result of this is that some of Marx's early writings, particularly his *1844 Manuscripts*, exhibit strong traces of the very Hegelian style that had at first repelled Marx. Another result is that many aspects of Marx's early positive thought developed out of internal criticisms of Hegelian concepts—as in the case of the 'universal class', already mentioned in Chapter 1. To be sure, Marx came to his reading of Hegel with strong preconceptions, but they were somewhat unrefined; grappling with the powerful mystifications, as Marx regarded them, of Hegel's all-embracing system, while utilizing its valuable methodological techniques, enabled Marx gradually to clarify and systematize his own thinking.

Among Hegel's philosophical remains are works on logic, his *Phenomenology of Spirit* [or . . . *of Mind*—the German word *Geist* stands for both], his *Philosophy of Right* [or . . . *of Law*—a similar situation obtains in the case of the German word *Recht*], and his *Philosophy of History*. The contents of each of these, which are interrelated in numerous ways, had some major effect on the philosophy of Marx, and I shall consider them in turn.

Neither Hegel's massive *Science of Logic* nor his so-called 'lesser *Logic*' contains much material that the average teacher of a course in logic today would find familiar or even relevant to his concerns. The same could be said concerning the teacher of classical (Aristotelian-based) logic in Hegel's or Marx's time. Hegel was aware of this, and regarded the usual logic texts as exercises in superficiality. The facts that the principal divisions—triadic in number, as is the case with most of Hegel's categorial schemata—of his system of logic are 'being', 'essence', and 'notion' and that the numerous subdivisions abound with such terms as 'ground', 'flux', 'mechanism', and 'chemism' gives some indication of the enormous distance that separates Hegel's conception of logic from the more ordinary one.

We need not, however, explore the intricacies of this system in order to obtain some sense of Marx's debt to it. What Hegel understands by 'logic' is essentially an explanatory method, supposed to be particularly fruitful because reflective of the actual structure of the world. The method that is common to both Marx and Hegel usually goes by the name of 'dialectics'; we may stick with this terminology for the moment, even though there are some technical reasons for questioning whether this label accurately characterizes all the philosophy of either Hegel or Marx. Since we shall consider this method, as Marx uses it, in some detail in the next chapter, we can be brief here. What Marx inherited from Hegel's studies in 'logic' was, above all, an awareness of the often sharp distinction between the appearances of things and their 'essences', or true natures, a recognition of the transitoriness of all describable states of affairs, a view that new systems and structures are generally produced by the intensification, to the point of conflict, of oppositions ('contradictions') within previously existing structures, and, finally, a commitment to a painstaking procedure of organizing data that involves beginning with highly abstract and general terms (e.g., value, commodity) and then tracing the interrelationships among particular phenomena (e.g., the exchange-value at a certain period of a given quantity of human labour-power, treated as a commodity) that are instances of these generalities, until a complex account of a concrete whole emerges. The conscious employment of these techniques is, surprisingly, more pronounced in Marx's later writings than in his earlier, allegedly 'more Hegelian' works. In a letter to Engels in 1858, Marx credited a recent re-reading of Hegel's *Logic* with facilitating his method of presenting his ideas. (In the same letter, he speaks of wishing some day to write a monograph in which he would exposit the 'rational' aspects of Hegel's method simply and straightforwardly, for the ordinary intelligent reader.)

In no other writing is the mystical part of Hegelianism, against which Marx rebelled, so dramatically revealed as in the *Phenomenology of Spirit*; but it too contributed much of a positive nature to Marx's philosophy. The *Phenomenology* is a systematically arranged study of different attitudes or stages of consciousness, from the most 'immediate' (i.e. unreflective) one of the simplest sense perception to the most advanced complexities of thought. Although he does not always make his case very persuasively, it is Hegel's contention that the inadequacy of each of his stages in turn somehow forces the mind, by a kind of inner logic, to abandon this stage in favour of the next, until the final stage of 'Absolute Spirit' has been reached. From this ultimate perspective, which is that of Hegel's philosophy, the mind is able to survey the path that it has taken in its development, recognizing both that each previous stage was necessary and that each had to be transcended, and that the active force throughout the entire process has been nothing other than itself (though it could not see this in the earlier stages). References abound throughout the book to actual movements and events in the history of Western thought, such as Stoicism and medieval Christianity, but the structure of the *Phenomenology* is not intended to reproduce, step by step, the history either of any single mind or of a civilization; its transitions and its ordering are ideal, not biographical. At the end it becomes clear that the Absolute Spirit is to be identified with God—a somewhat unorthodox divinity, to be sure, immanent in the world, which has caused itself to evolve by means of the actual minds of individuals and of the 'spirits' (this metaphor of ordinary language is to be taken literally in Hegel) of various epochs of civilization. Marx utterly rejected, from the beginning of his acquaintance with Hegel, this conception of a spiritual agency, finding no evidence for it, and considerable evidence that material forces of various sorts shape the world as we know it.

Nevertheless, many of the *Phenomenology*'s detailed descriptions of complicated mental postures remain masterful. Of these, none has been more influential on both Marx and later Marxism than the section known as 'Master and Servant', or, more archaically, 'Lordship and Bondage'. Within the scheme of the book, this section is pivotal in accounting for the difference between the merely animal level of consciousness and the selfconsciousness that is characteristically human. At the level of abstraction at which it is written, the passage could be taken to refer to two aspects of a single human consciousness as well as to an interaction between two consciousnesses (although the latter interpretation seems less forced), and the use of the term's 'master' and 'servant' is obviously intended as a metaphorical aid to comprehension (we might think, for instance, of a 'servile' mental attitude and its opposite) rather than as a literal reference to actual legal relationships. Hegel maintains that fully human selfconsciousness is attainable only through a process of becoming 'recognized' by others, and that this can be achieved only through struggle. 'Struggle to the death', in the limiting case, arrests the entire process, since one of the antagonists ceases to exist. Short of this, the radically unequal master-servant relationship takes hold, and both 'master' and 'servant' attitudes then evolve further. At the end, a reversal of roles occurs: the master comes to realize that, in order to continue as master, he is totally dependent on the servant's acting as a servant; whereas the servant, after passing through a period of extreme anxiety in which he fears for his life, comes to realize that it is only through his labour as servant that the entire relationship can be maintained. In all the phases of this account, as throughout Hegel's philosophy, the concept of 'alienation', regarded as an essential part of any process of development, plays a major role: consciousness must become alien or foreign to itself, so to speak (as in the extreme case of the servant's fearing for his very life at the point at which the sense of dependency

B

is strongest in him), in order subsequently to 'put itself back together' at a stage of fuller self-awareness.

Marx was greatly influenced by the Hegelian view of the world as pervaded by conflict; however, he did not accept the claim that this situation was perpetual and ineluctable. Relationships with most other human beings were necessarily 'alienating' in a class-divided and competitive society, Marx felt, but a radically different form of society was conceivable. Hegel's view that alienation was eternally necessary stemmed from his pervasive idealism: if the human being is essentially spirit, yearning to be self-enclosed and autonomous but incapable of being so, then any involvement with other spirits, especially since this involvement has to take place by means of bodies and other material objects, is inevitably a sort of self-negation, a degradation. But Marx considered human beings to be material, natural entities, albeit of a very special kind. He seized upon Hegel's insistence that it was the *labour*, the 'shaping and fashioning' activity, of the servant in the *Phenomenology* that made the world of human relationships continue to turn. In the fact that Hegel was satisfied with a mere resolution in consciousness, in philosophical thought, rather than in the 'real world', of the unequal dominance-subordination relationship that he had described so strikingly, Marx saw epitomized the entire function of German academic philosophy as at once mystifier of reality and ideological justifier of the existing socio-political order. He says as much in an early essay on Hegel's philosophy as a whole.

In the *Philosophy of Right*, this role of traditional philosophy is played out in even more straightforward fashion. Hegel had become the official philosopher of the Prussian state by the time of his writing this book. In it (especially in the last and longest section, that on 'the State', which occupies a position *nearly*, but not quite, parallel to that of 'Absolute Spirit' in the *Phenomenology*) the basic institutions of that monarchical regime, greatly systematized and idealized, are in effect paraded before the reader as embodiments of the most rational and fully developed modern political order. Many commentators have therefore found it easy to dismiss the *Philosophy of Right* as mere reactionary drivel, but they are mistaken, and Marx himself devoted three months of 1843 to a paragraph-by-paragraph analysis of parts of it.

Marx's principal critical concern in this study was to demonstrate, by a detailed examination of Hegel's own language, that the political institutions described were the products of prior material conditions rather than of some imaginary, self-realizing 'Idea'. More specifically, Marx attempted to refute Hegel's contention that the State—i.e., the organs of the national government—really performed the service of harmonizing and reconciling the conflicting particular interest-groups whose existence was most prominent at the level of social life that Hegel called 'civil society'. Rather, Marx tried to show, we can see Hegel himself admitting between the lines that the government ('State') merely facilitates the continued dominance of those interest-groups that have the greater power within civil society.

Of equal importance is the extent of Marx's acceptance of Hegel's categories in describing the modern social world; the fact that Hegel complacently considered this world to be as ideal as possible (although he was extremely careful to acknowledge that he was treating only the best aspects of the modern state and placing them in their best light, discarding all its daily occurrences of particular inequities as inessential to his rational reconstruction) should not blind us to the subtleties of his account. Hegel's anatomy of civil society, which is the translation of *bürgerliche Gesellschaft* and in turn retranslatable as 'bourgeois society', is especially rich. Individuals in their capacity as 'burghers', the businessmen and workers of the increasingly city-orientated form of social life that began to develop in the late Middle Ages as a replacement for feudal society, look first to the satisfaction of their own interests rather than to any common interest. Their activities are therefore characterized by narrow egoism and 'particularity'—terms that have pejorative connotations in Hegel's vocabulary. Political economy is the new science, Hegel says, that has arisen to delineate, with remarkable precision and detail, the 'system of needs' of this aspect of social life; this science operates at the level of mere 'understanding' (as opposed to 'reason'), imparting to the mechanisms of civil society a 'show' of rationality—once again, a subtly pejorative characterization. Near the end of his treatment of 'civil society', in a few brief paragraphs, Hegel nearly removes his mask of optimism entirely as he writes of the inevitable tendency of modern civil societies, driven by internally generated economic forces that they cannot control, to become polarized in such a way as to develop a large pauper class and then, in order to stave off the worst effects of such a development, to turn their attention to overseas colonization, or what would today be called imperialism. But soon after this Hegel introduces the State, with much blaring of trumpets ('the State is the actuality of the ethical Idea [. . .] the State is absolutely rational [. . .].'), and most readers are moved to forget the prophetic vision of a far from ideal future to which they have just been made privy.

Not so Marx; it is no exaggeration to say that the essence of his conception of capitalism, though with no supporting evidence, is to be found scattered in the few pages of Hegel's treatment of 'civil society'. But Marx, unlike Hegel, found no solution to the dissonances of that society in the apparatus of the modern State; rather, as we shall see in Chapter 7, Marx's solution can best be called 'post-political'. It is often forgotten that Hegel himself, despite the apparent conviction with which he sometimes speaks of modern civilization as the most ideal of societies and his own time as the best of all possible times, does not conclude the *Philosophy of Right* with his idealized Prussia in a position exactly parallel to that of 'Absolute Spirit' in the *Phenomenology*; rather, he maintains that world history is a kind of higher court of judgement in which even the best of states will be judged and (presumably) found wanting. This claim, stripped of its metaphorical flourishes, was also of great influence on the philosophy of Marx.

Hegel's *Philosophy of History* (actually a collation of notes from his lectures that was first published shortly after his death) was for a long time probably the best known of his writings in the English-speaking world. Its essential premiss is that the mainstream of world history, moving from the 'Oriental World' of ancient Persia, India, etc., on through Greece and Rome to a climax in 'Germanic civilization' (by which Hegel means something like 'Western Christendom'—i.e., all the European nations created out of the old barbarian tribes), has developed progressively towards more rational and freer social forms. This does not exclude the occurrence of many backings, meanderings, and periods of stagnation, but these are seen, as in the case of inequities in the *Philosophy of Right*, to be 'inessential'. The book's surface tone is one of optimism, rivalling that of the eighteenth-century Enlightenment, but its undertones are those of deep, somewhat romantic tragedy; one can understand its appeal to the Victorian temperament. For example, in one of his best-known turns of phrase, Hegel describes history as a 'slaughter-bench' to which innocent victims are brought in the name of a higher purpose. But the workings of history for Hegel cannot appropriately be judged in terms of ordinary moral categories.

The normative category of freedom, on the other hand, is the key to its comprehension. With an unwonted simplicity, Hegel provides a schema for labelling the main stages of history in accordance with the prevalence of freedom in them: in the Oriental World, it can be said that 'one is free', the one individual in question being the despot; in Greece and Rome, 'some are free', and some are slaves; and in the modern world, especially in its latest phase since the French Revolution, 'all are free'. Once again, as in the rest of his thought, Hegel attributes ultimate causal agency in history to a self-developing spiritual entity—'history', he says, 'is not only not without God', but 'is essentially His work'. The mechanism of this process, as Hegel conceives it, is captured in a clever turn of phrase that has become more memorable because it is less redolent of theological meanings than some others: the 'cunning of reason'. Reason carries out its cosmic goals, Hegel contends, by means of the private ambitions and passions of individuals, especially of the rare, particularly influential, 'world-historical individuals', the Alexanders and the Napoleons. Events do not turn out in accordance with the original projects of the latter, who in the end can be seen to have been reason's instruments.

Marx eliminated from his own philosophical conception of history all the blatantly theological trappings of Hegel's. He occasionally showed an implicit awareness, moreover, of the cultural provinciality of Hegel's viewpoint. But there was much, probably too much, of it that Marx retained. The recognition that the particular projects of individuals are often 'counter-finalized' through a sequence of complex historical events was a useful one for Marx, who showed much less temptation than Hegel himself to exaggerate the importance of individuals in moulding history. Marx took a great interest in the Hegelian criterion of degrees and kinds of freedom in marking off historical periods—e.g., that of the feudal serf from that of the modern labourer working under free contract—but of course he dissented totally from Hegel's contention that the condition of the 'free labourer' was optimal in terms of the possibilities of free human action. Marx's single most pervasive inheritance from Hegel's philosophy of history, however, was an attitudinal one: an attitude of optimism that easily surpassed Hegel's own. In Hegel's thought, such an attitude, though tempered by sentimentality over history's 'necessary' tragedies, had a systematic philosophical basis in the conception of history as teleological, purposive. In the philosophy of Marx, the existence of no entity is hypothesized to guarantee that everything will work out for the best, and Marx is more scrupulous than was Hegel himself in avoiding the importation of moral categories, such as 'good' and 'best', into accounts of historical developments. Yet Marx's expectation, inherited from the greatest of the idealist thinkers, that something 'better' is bound to succeed what we have at present, exerts a considerable colouring effect at crucial points.

(c) Contemporaries

Internal criticism of Hegel's thought was a common activity among the keenest young philosophers in Marx's student days, and Marx was among the liveliest critics. The intellectual atmosphere that pervaded the loosely knit group known as the Young Hegelians, therefore, was obviously of considerable importance in shaping the philosophy of Marx at a critical stage in its development. Marx devoted many reams of paper—some published during his lifetime (notably, *The Holy Family*), much not published until decades later —to criticizing the shortcomings in the thought of several of his contemporaries or near-contemporaries in this group.

Marx learned something of value to him from many of these individuals. To his early academic patron Bruno Bauer, for instance, Marx owed the opportunity of working through his own ideas about the inadequacy of all merely political solutions to social problems, since it was Bauer's moderately 'progressive' but still reformist views concerning Jewish political emancipation that Marx analysed and criticized in his long, tortuous, and somewhat confused review, *On The Jewish Question*. Through exchanges of correspondence with the well-heeled Arnold Ruge, whose financial assistance in founding the short-lived, ill-fated *German-French Annals* provided the occasion for Marx's moving to Paris, Marx clarified his sense of the drift of current political events and intensified his own resolution to become a political activist. From Moses Hess, the 'Communist Rabbi' (whose connection with the original Young Hegelians was peripheral), Marx learned a good deal about socialism, and thus became more convinced of the need to undertake a critique of political economy. In the philosophy of Max Stirner, whose *The Ego and His Own* he and Engels attacked savagely in *The German Ideology*, Marx saw the logical outcome of an extreme subjective individualism, and thenceforth guarded himself more carefully against such a world-view. But two related developments stand out most, in historical retrospect, in Marx's intricate intellectual and personal relationships with the Young Hegelians: first, a gradual shift of emphasis from religious to political to economic criticism; and second, the rejection of Feuerbach's philosophy.

It was on the subject of religion that, generally speaking, the Young Hegelians first concentrated their writing activity, and it was the question whether to remain Christians, albeit theologically unorthodox ones, or to abandon Christian beliefs entirely that divided the movement into right and left wings. Hegel himself had always contended that he was a Christian, and he had been a churchgoer (in the established Lutheran church of Prussia), but the legacy of his philosophy of religion, like that of the remainder of his system, was in fact highly ambiguous. From the standpoint of his philosophy, he had effected a rational reconstruction of traditional Christian doctrines. To mention only the most basic difference, Hegel's deity was far more immanent, far less transcendent to the human world, than the mainstream of historical Christianity had held its deity to be. There are strong grounds for maintaining, against Hegel himself, that his philosophy is a disguised atheism, if 'theism' refers to belief in a traditional Christian (or Jewish) God. With the publication in 1835 of *The Life of Jesus*, by an erstwhile student of Hegel's, David Strauss, who ascribed a mythical basis to the stories contained in the Christian Scriptures, a process began whereby most of the already tenuous links between neo-Hegelianism and the Christian religion as it was actually understood by its ordinary devotees were eventually to be severed. This process was in effect completed, at least if we are to believe Engels's account of the atmosphere of the period, with the publication of Ludwig Feuerbach's *The Essence of Christianity* in 1841. Feuerbach, a highly respected, somewhat older, Young Hegelian not then residing in Berlin, not only proclaimed his atheism proudly, but also broke (to a far greater degree than Marx himself) with the Hegelian philosophical style. In *Ludwig Feuerbach and the End of Classical German Philosophy*, written after Marx's death and accompanied by the first published version of Marx's famous *Theses on Feuerbach*, Engels describes the general reaction as having been one of great mental release and liberation.

To Marx himself, who had never been intensely religious, the proclamation of atheism against Hegel and the established order but in keeping with most of his peers could hardly have seemed particularly challenging as a long-term intellectual endeavour. In several of his early writings, he contends that the criticism of religion would be the starting-point of critical philosophical activity but not its ultimate goal, and he argues, employing the now shopworn phrase about 'the opium of the people', that the continued existence of religious practices in a modern society is symptomatic of a widespread lack of need-satisfaction, itself due to other causes, in that society. Marx thus provides a theoretical justification for the general increase of interest in political questions, in part the result of an intensified effort at repressing dissent and unorthodoxy on the part of the Prussian regime, that is detectable in the writings of his philosophical contemporaries during the early 1840s. During the same few years, however, Marx's own intellectual interest evolved in such a way that the Young Hegelian movement as such ceased to exert much influence over him. Events in his life—his experience as a journalist, his introduction to large-scale workers' movements for the first time in Paris, and the beginning of his close collaboration with Engels—combined to ensure this outcome, in any case, but his repudiation of Feuerbach is the most clear-cut intellectual manifestation of it.

The Essence of Christianity, in which Feuerbach anticipates Freud by contending that religion is explicable as mankind's worship of a highly idealized version of its own best qualities, collectively projected onto an illusory object named God, may not have had as much influence on Marx's development as did a later, shorter Feuerbachian essay, 'Preliminary Theses for the Reform of Philosophy'. The title, *Theses on Feuerbach*, parodies Feuerbach's later title rather than his earlier one. Feuerbach was convinced that the tradition of German idealism, focused in Hegel's 'Spirit'-oriented philosophy but common to a great many thinkers of the period, provided an ultimate refuge for the other-worldly conceptual framework of classical Christianity, now greatly rarefied and refined. Feuerbach was a materialist almost by instinct, revelling in talk about human love and the satisfaction of appetites. Phenomena such as these, he contended, ought to be the objects of philosophical concern. As a means of bringing about this reform he proposed an analytic approach to Hegel (and to idealism in general) known as the 'transformative method', whereby one attempts to dissolve the empty abstractions that occupy the subject-positions in crucial sentences in idealist writings (of the general form: 'The Idea [Spirit, God, etc.] expresses the attributes x, y, and z') and move the predicates or attributes to the subject-positions. When the idealist says, for instance, that God expresses Himself in the various forms of human love, the Feuerbachian shows that the various manifestations of human love have an autonomous existence and bring about various results in the world. Marx employed this informal, heuristic method to some effect, particularly in his extended critique of Hegel's *Philosophy of Right*, rearranging entire Hegelian paragraphs to eliminate references to the alleged agency of 'Spirit' or 'the Idea', and thus produce passable empirical descriptions of political phenomena.

Feuerbach himself never evinced much interest in politics or history in his writings, and this disturbed Marx even during the period in which, in Engels's words, 'We all [were] Feuerbachians'. Nevertheless, at this time Feuerbach's philosophy had a considerable influence over Marx's social thought, as illustrated by the latter's adoption of the neologism for the generic word 'man', on which Feuerbach laid so much emphasis: 'species-being' (*Gattungswesen* in German). The idea behind the employment of this word was roughly that the most salient characteristic distinguishing human beings from other animals (a traditional philosophical problem for materialists, more than for dualists or idealists) was humans' capacity to think of themselves as a species, having certain general and perfectible qualities common to all, and having a history. This conception, very useful for Feuerbach in defending his argument that Christianity could be radically transformed into a quasi-religion of humanity if Christians would only realize that they had in fact always been worshipping the idealized positive attributes of the human race under the mystifying, superfluous name of 'God', was helpful to Marx in clarifying his own notion of an harmonious human community as it might exist at some future time. One of the forms of alienation that Marx claimed, in his *1844 Manuscripts*, to find in the society of his day was alienation of individuals from their 'species-being'. Like Feuerbach, in other words, Marx held that humanity was, in fact, 'species-being', but that individuals were generally either unaware of this or, if aware, unable to live and act in accordance with this awareness, because of social conditions. But the scope of the offensive social conditions, and hence of the effort needed to overcome them, was much narrower in Feuerbach's thought, confined as it was largely to religious practices, than in Marx's.

In the *Theses on Feuerbach*, written (though, as I have noted, not published) in 1845, Marx changed roles from one of admirer to one of critic. Subsequently, he and Engels jointly wrote (but left unfinished) *The German Ideology*, in which Feuerbach the 'ideologist' held pride of place as the object of polemical attack in the first section (although, in fact, the text of that section itself contains relatively little direct reference to him). What is the significance of this shift? Some have seen in it the sign of a complete break in Marx's thought, but that is surely too extreme. Between them Marx and Engels make relatively clear the pattern of Marx's intellectual deveopment at this time. Marx had decided that Feuerbach's failure to attend sufficiently to political questions was more serious, more revelatory of fundamental shortcomings in his philosophy, than Marx had at first admitted: criticism of religious practices and thinking, Marx was more convinced than ever, did not by itself ferret out the most significant causal factors accounting for social structures. Moreover, Feuerbach had, according to Marx, underestimated something of value while rejecting much of the dross in Hegel's idealism. This valuable element was a conception of human action as being something different in kind from a simply passive, billiard-ball-like reaction to external pressures: an *adequate* materialism of the sort that Marx wished to espouse would have to focus upon this phenomenon of human action, which Marx in passing called 'sensuous human activity, *praxis*'. As a result of this deficiency in his thought, Marx now maintained, Feuerbach's proposed reform of philosophy had not been nearly radical enough; Feuerbach still regarded philosophy as passively observing or contemplating objects at a distance, rather than as an activity that was at once theoretical and practical, engaged in bringing about changes in the world. Finally, Marx was now anxious to repudiate the use to which Feuerbach had put the language of 'essences', particularly with respect to notions about an 'essence of man'. Henceforth, Marx was to eschew references to 'species-being', for he had concluded that the essential (in the acceptable sense of the term) characteristics of human society differed from one historical period to another, and that to speak of an eternal human essence militated against social change. Specifically, Feuerbach's proposal that we worship the highest possibilities of an idealized humanity, with its emphasis on 'love' and similar abstractions as the 'essence' of his own radically reconceived version of Christianity, had the effect of turning attention away from the prevalence of class conflict and of other relationships of dominance and subordination in the actual present world.

At this crucial point in his career, then, Marx was selective, rather than wholesale, in his rejection of elements of his philosophical past. What was probably most significant about his repudiation of Feuerbach was the new clarity with which it provided him, by way of contrast with this distinguished contemporary, concerning the aim or purpose of his own future theorizing; I have already discussed this point in Chapter 1. Although, in breaking with Feuerbach, Marx gave up misleading talk about 'species-being', this did not entail his abandoning the concept of 'alienation' in his later work, as it was once fashionable for certain Marxologists to maintain. In discarding the idea of a fixed 'human essence', Marx in no wise despaired of efforts to discover the 'essences', as opposed to the surface appearances', of phenomena—efforts which (even if one finds fault with this particular terminology) are indispensable for theoretical explanation. If anything, Marx's criticism of Feuerbach (in the first of the famous *Theses*) on the topics of the latter's methodology and of his conception of human beings constitutes a reaffirmation, as Marx himself says, of certain Hegelian insights, though held within a materialist framework, from Marx's past. By virtue of these Hegelian elements, Marx's philosophy always retained a very different flavour, or exhibited a very different style, both from that of the eighteenth-century materialists (Helvétius, Holbach, *et al.*) with whom he frequently contrasted himself and from that of other nineteenth-century aspirants to positive, scientific truth who shared his abhorrence of idealist mystification. Feuerbach's own later writings on religion, by comparison, are defences of a typical, straightforward atheist position from which his earlier 'dialectical' recognition that some grain of truth, though expressed in a one-sided, oblique fashion, attaches to traditional religious practices has almost vanished; as a result, these works are now of little inerest except to specialists.

With one exception, the philosophy of Marx ceased to be influenced by his contemporaries to any meaningful extent after his move to London in 1849. That exception, of course, was Friedrich Engels. Although Engels himself grandly accorded to Marx all the laurels in originating and developing the theory known as Marxism, assigning to himself only the roles of editor, popularizer and occasional adviser in areas (such as the natural sciences and military science) in which Engels was more knowledgeable, this account will not quite do. We may set aside for the moment, if we wish, the important historical fact that Marxism as it came to be understood by the late nineteenth-century and twentieth-century reading publics was very largely a Marxism filtered through the pen of Engels, whose gift for popular exposition was so much greater (or at least so much more often exercised) than Marx's. We may assume, if we please, that Engels's massive editorial work on the unpublished portions of *Capital* after Marx's death never deviated in outcome from what Marx himself would have wished. But we can hardly fly in the face of common sense to the extent of denying that Engels had *any* active role in elaborating the conceptions and arguments to be found in the important writings that he and Marx jointly authored. And if he played a role in these, then why not in other parts of Marx's philosophy as well?

The problem then becomes one of finding a method for separating the peculiarly Engelsian elements from the rest. In the last analysis, of course, there is no authoritative way of doing this completely. The collaboration of Engels with Marx was extraordinarily close, and I know of no point in their extensive extant correspondence at which they appear consciously to be at loggerheads over any matter of great philosophical importance. (They occasionally disagree, to be sure, in their estimates of current events, although even in such matters disagreement is very rare.) Nevertheless, they were men of very different backgrounds, temperaments, and life-styles, and of somewhat divergent intellectual interests. Engels had not prepared for an academic career but had come into contact with 'Young Hegelian' intellectuals of Marx's circle (though not with Marx himself, who had already left) during his brief period of service as a military officer in Berlin. A reluctant but efficient businessman (in his father's textile firm) by profession, Engels was more eclectic in his research and readier to construct sweeping syntheses about the cosmos than was Marx. These qualities must surely have had an effect on Marx's own thinking.

To Engels, rather than to Marx, falls the honour of having published the first full-length book that is recognizably 'Marxist' in orientation: it is his *The Condition of the Working Class in England in 1844*, the outcome of research that he undertook when first stationed in Manchester, just prior to his becoming well acquainted with Marx himself. In this work, sentences containing empirical supporting data are more numerous than sentences of theoretical analysis, but the beginnings of a radical, proto-Marxist critique of capitalism are clearly discernible. The ideas contained in this book, conveyed verbally by Engels during Marx's stay in Paris, made a great impression on Marx, as did Engels's penchant for relying on statistical data.

It would be a mistake, however, to depict the complementarity between Marx and Engels in later years as one of theoretician and statistician. Both were able theorists, but Marx was the more cautious of the two. Engels, for example, frequently subscribes to very strong versions of value relativism, denying that the meanings of such terms as 'justice', 'freedom', and even 'truth' are identical from one society to the next, and sometimes even putting into doubt their identity from one person to the next; at such times, he seems oblivious of the philosophical objection that it is inconsistent to make absolute claims concerning the non-existence of absolutes. Reading Engels, one is left with the impression of a greater tolerance of other positions than one has from reading Marx, precisely because of Engels's greater affinity for relativism. But this impression is deceptive; upon closer analysis, I think, Engels will be found to be much more dogmatic on the whole than Marx—however breezily his dogmatism may be expressed—in asserting propositions about the ultimate nature of the social world. (Correspondingly, Engels was also more authoritarian in his vision of a future socialist society.)

Nor was it the social world alone that Engels embraced within his generalizations; he was, to a far greater extent than Marx, an inveterate ontologist, inclined to generalize concerning the ultimate nature of reality. Unlike Marx, who knew little other than what Engels told him concerning important new discoveries and theoretical developments in the natural sciences, Engels immersed himself in such subjects, and greatly enjoyed speculating about them. This characteristic of Engels certainly exerted influence over Marx's later philosophy.

Engels was attracted to a conception of science, the reigning one among scientists and philosophers of science at the time, as consisting of the discovery and elaboration of objective, verifiable laws that are supposed to govern the behaviour of every particle in the universe. The set of such laws is assumed, in this conception, to be unique and all-embracing, so that ultimately there will be found to be no fundamental difference in kind between the natural and the social sciences. Implicit in an adherence to such a conception is a commitment to a strong, universal determinism. So we find Engels frequently speculating about the age-old question whether, and if so in what sense, human action can be free in a deterministic world.

The principal route to attempting to answer this, for Engels, is to insist (as Hegel also had, but in a much more complex fashion) on the supposedly dialectical character of the relationship between freedom and determinism. The presumed resolution thus effected is primarily verbal, but it indicates the reason why Engels considers his own conception of scientific laws to be both different from and superior to that of most of his (loosely speaking, 'positivist') contemporaries. The key term is 'dialectics'. Previous philosophies of science, according to Engels, have been either insufficiently rigorous or experimentally based (as in the case of Hegel), or else insufficiently dialectical. With the proclamation of the Darwinian theory of evolution, which made a great stir among scientists and the ordinary public during the time when Marx was working diligently to prepare *Capital* for publication, Engels saw a triumphant and conclusive demonstration of the superiority of dialectical methodology. To Engels, non-dialectical method (the so-called 'narrow, metaphysical mode' of thinking) is deficient in failing to give sufficient weight to considerations of development and of interrelationships; but the plausibility of Darwinism depends on just such considerations. Ergo, Marxism, the dialectical social science *par excellence,* is vindicated by association.

A letter has been found in which Marx himself recommends to Engels that he elaborate on the supposed parallel between Darwinism in the natural sciences and Marxism in the sciences of society. The occasion was an invitation that Engels had received to review *Capital,* Volume I (recently published for the first time), for a German newspaper. The opportunity was a splendid one, and Engels had written to Marx for advice concerning the best line of argument to take in praising Marx's virtues. Marx's reply is unabashedly cynical, suggesting that Engels draw the Marx-Darwin parallel as a means of settling several scores at once and also promoting sales. But Engels came in time to regard the parallel with utmost seriousness, and in this development lies the crux of the issue concerning Engels's most important influence over the philosophy of Marx and over later Marxism.

Marx never explicitly dissented from the conception of the sciences, including the social sciences as a part of them, upon which Engels elaborated in several of his writings. On the contrary, he sometimes made suggestions to Engels on the subject, and at several points in *Capital,* both in the original Volume I and particularly in the very rich and informative Afterword to the second German edition, Marx described his own discovery of the 'laws' of capitalist production in a fashion very much in keeping with this conception. But there is little doubt of its having become more prominent in Marx's later philosophy by comparison even with the writings of his middle years, and so we must raise the question (without hoping ever to resolve it definitively) whether this evolution was due primarily to Engels's influence on Marx. At any rate, it creates difficulties for anyone attempting to understand the philosophy of Marx, since the Engelsian 'scientific' conception of what Marxism is turns out to be incompatible, in important respects, with an alternative conception or conceptions that Marx himself sometimes appears to have favoured, and yet Marx wrote very little of a systematic nature that is of use in resolving the matter; we shall see this in detail later. It is also worthwhile noting, in passing, that aspects of Engels's conception of the 'objective laws' of science now appear outmoded to a generation that is more aware of the complexities of physical scientific theory, so that the adoption of his views on the subject as official doctrine in certain educational systems has had a retarding effect.

Among Engels's lengthy notes on science and scientific method that were published posthumously under the title *The Dialectics of Nature* there is a reference to three 'laws' which Engels proposes as the most general of all: the transformation of quantity into quality and the reverse, the interpenetration of opposites, and the negation of the negation. The proposal, it is clear from the context, is not intended to be taken dogmatically and categorically, but it has in fact often been taken this way by later writers of textbooks on the bastardized version of Marx's philosophy that goes by the name of 'dialectical materialism'. Marx's own writings do not lend themselves with such ease to this sort of misuse: he was temperamentally and intellectually less inclined to indulge in the sweeping generalities about the universe, however qualified by such phrases as 'more or less', that are so characteristic of his collaborator. Another passage in *The Dialectics of Nature* clearly reveals the difference in perspective that separates the two: in it Engels discusses the eventual destruction of the planet Earth, the history of which appears as a temporary episode in the history of the universe. Such reflections were, to judge from the available literary evidence, very much in keeping with his inclination to think in cosmic and cosmological terms and very little in keeping with Marx's primary interests.

In a letter written late in his life, to the editorial board of a

Russian newspaper, Marx rejected the interpretation of Marxism as 'a general historico-philosophical theory, the supreme virtue of which consists in being super-historical'. Elsewhere, however (e.g., in *The Communist Manifesto*, a joint effort of which the final draft was Marx's), Marx himself lends some credence to this interpretation (without the final clause, of course), and Engels does so frequently. Some unclarity remains, therefore, not only concerning the extent of Engels's influence on Marx's philosophy, but also concerning Marx's own understanding of the nature of his philosophy. However, we have succeeded in bringing to light some of the divergences between Marx and Engels that enable us to make progress towards settling these questions. Bearing in mind both the frequent value of Engel's popularizations of Marx's thought and the need always to retain some scepticism about their faithfulness to the original, we are now prepared to begin analysing Marx's philosophy proper by discussing its methodological component.

3 Marx's Method

In coming to grips with the philosophy of Marx, a great deal hinges on understanding his method. 'Dialectics' is the name usually given to it, and this is accurate as far as it goes. However, a wide variety of interpretations can be given to the notion of dialectical methodology, and indeed Marx's own very scattered references to it permit of just such a variety. Moreover, there are elements both of Marx's research and of his thought that do not readily lend themselves to being caught within the net of dialectical method, however widely cast. Or if, alternatively, one does develop an extremely broad conception of dialectics, then of course it ceases to be at all distinctive as a method. Nevertheless, some of the characteristic features of dialectical method, even if they are not the exclusive property of dialecticians, are indispensable to the philosophy of Marx and useful for advancing the sorts of aims that he had in mind. Or so I shall argue here.

Methodology is generally considered a dry subject. On the other hand, the word 'dialectics' conjures up exciting thoughts of the magical and the mystical, of objects metamorphosing themselves in a fashion that eludes description in coherent language. The conception of a dialectical method, then, implies some unification of attitudinal opposites—a typically dialectical way of thinking. The desire to bring together opposites is fundamental to the dialectician because of an even more primary goal: that of comprehensiveness. The dialectician wishes to bring all aspects of the subject that he or she is investigating within the scope of a single, systematic account; thus, dialectical writing is filled with such adjectives as 'one-sided', 'incomplete', and 'abstract' to characterize less comprehensive, presumably undialectical positions. The dialectician assumes that non-dialectical thinkers have made the error of taking a fragment of the reality under investigation for the whole; implicit in this is the further assumption that reality itself is both fragmented and dialectical, but that the dialectical method is superior to others in that it can account for both fragments and whole, whereas the others can account only for the fragments. All these features—a curious combination of dryness, due to the appearance of proclaiming something trite and obvious, with magical excitement, a strong effort to be all-embracing, a critique of other positions for being partial, and a statement about the nature of reality—appear in the following passages from Hegel, which are worth citing at length:

[. . .] In its true and proper character, Dialectic is the very nature and essence of everything predicated by the mere understanding,—the law of things and of the finite as a whole [. . .] By Dialectic is meant the indwelling tendency outwards by which the one-sidedness and limitation of the predicates of understanding is seen in its true light, and shown to be the negation of them. For anything to be finite is just to suppress itself and put itself aside. Thus understood the Dialectical principle constitutes the life and soul of scientific progress [. . .].

However reluctant Understanding may be to admit the action of Dialectic, we must not suppose that the recognition of its existence is peculiarly confined to the philosopher. It would be truer to say that Dialectic gives expression to a law which is felt in all other grades of consciousness, and in general experience. Everything that surrounds us may be viewed as an instance of Dialectic. We are aware that everything finite, instead of being stable and ultimate, is rather changeable and transient; and this is exactly what we mean by that Dialectic of the finite, by which the finite, as implicitly other than what it is, is forced beyond its own immediate or natural being to turn suddenly into its opposite. (*The Logic of Hegel*, p. 147 and 149–50.)

In the next sentence Hegel goes on to make a point about the attributes of God, which serves to warn us of the theistic context in which his insistence on the application of dialectics to 'the finite' must be viewed. Beyond the finite, he implies, there is an area of reality that cannot be fully comprehended even by the method of dialectics.

If one troubles to read the above passages closely one can, even if one has had no previous acquaintance with Hegel's writing, distil a considerable amount of meaningful information from them. But they are also typified by an open-endedness, a vagueness, and, despite constant protestations to the contrary throughout Hegel's works, an abstractness that render what he has to say about dialectic highly elusive. The mere possession of these qualities is not by itself sufficient to cause a philosophical text to be adjudged worthless (although 'vagueness' does, it is true, usually connote something rather disreputable); one may, for instance, simply be forced to write abstractly in order to convey very abstract ideas. But these passages are useful for suggesting the depth of the difficulty that we face in providing a precise account of the meaning of the dialectical method, which Marx inherited from Hegel.

It is not the case that Marx ever wrote about dialectics in the Hegelian style, or that he ever entertained Hegelian notions about a realm of reality 'beyond the finite'. In fact, if the truth be told, Marx, like Hegel, published very little of an explicit nature concerning his dialectical method. There is one noteworthy exception to this—namely the final three or four pages of the Afterword to the second German edition of *Capital*, Volume I. But what Marx says here, apropos of the numerous and contradictory misinterpretations of his method that had appeared in reviews of his first edition, raises at least as many questions as it resolves.

Particularly irritating for someone looking for a definitive statement by Marx on the subject of his methodology is the fact that he resorts to the tactic of citing with approval—or at least with *apparent* approval—someone else's account of what he is doing. The individual in question was a reviewer for the *European Messenger* of St Petersburg, Russia, who began by deploring Marx's dialectical German method of presentation of his ideas, which he considered idealistic in form, while applauding the realism of his method of inquiry. Marx proceeds to quote at length from some of the more positive parts of the review, by way of responding to the negative criticism. Here are a few sentences:

The one thing which is of moment to Marx, is to find the law of the phenomena with whose investigation he is concerned; [. . .] of still greater moment to him is the law of their variation, of their development, i.e., of their transition from one form into another [. . .] Marx only troubles himself about one thing: to show, by rigid scientific investigation, the necessity of successive determinate orders of social conditions, and to establish, as impartially as possible, the facts that serve him for fundamental starting-points [. . .] Marx treats the social movement as a process of natural history, governed by laws not only independent of human will, consciousness, and intelligence, but rather, on the contrary, determining that will, consciousness, and intelligence [. . .]. In Marx's opinion, every historical period has laws of its own [. . .]. As soon as society has outlived a given period of development, and is passing over from one stage to another, it begins to be subject also to other laws. In a word, economic life offers us a phenomenon analogous to the history of evolution in other branches of biology [. . .]. (*Capital*, Vol. I, Afterword to the second German edition.)

Marx then proceeds to vindicate himself, in his own mind, by asking the following rhetorical question: 'Whilst the writer pictures what he takes to be actually my method, in this striking and (as far as concerns my own application) generous way, what else is he picturing but the dialectic method?' Of course, he adds, the methods of presentation and of inquiry must differ: the latter involves struggle and analysis, and if it has been successful in getting at the truth about the subject-matter, then the presentation may *appear* to be ideal and merely *a priori*. Marx's Afterword then concludes with the several paragraphs, mentioned in Chapter 2, in which he tries to summarize the complex relationship between his thought and Hegel's by saying that his own dialectic method is the 'direct opposite' of the latter's and by indulging in the famous metaphors concerning standing it right side up and extracting the rational kernel from the mystical shell.

What is probably clearest about Marx's remarks concerning the dialectical method on these pages is his conviction of its usefulness in calling attention to the changeable character of all existing systems and states of affairs, and hence to their vulnerability to criticism. This is all right, but it is not enough to explain dialectics adequately to anyone. On the other hand, the review passages cited by Marx complicate matters by introducing considerations of an ontological kind—e.g., the analogy between economic life and biological evolution—into the question of what Marx's dialectical method is. In Marx's defence, it can be said, of course, that he did not plan his Afterword as a definitive exposition of dialectics, but rather as a short, informal commentary on some of the early reactions to his book. Unfortunately, however, he never wrote a definite exposition; this, plus a few pages elsewhere, is all that we possess by way of direct discussion of the subject by Marx, and the rest must be reconstructed from the writings in which he is most obviously intending to use the dialectical method.

Probably the most spectacular instance of Marx's use of a technique that is readily identifiable as dialectical occurs in his overall plan of the three volumes of *Capital*. (His posthumously published *Theories of Surplus Value*, primarily an historical survey of some of the important political economists' views, is sometimes listed as a fourth volume of *Capital*, but that is a matter of editorial convenience, and irrelevant to present considerations.) A single page introducing Volume III makes it clear that the three volumes are intended by Marx to form a structured, systematic triad: Volume I dealt with the underlying factors of the capitalist system, which Marx calls, collectively, the 'sphere of production'; Volume II (which is, in fact, very dry, and the least philosophically rewarding by most standards) treated of various aspects of exchange (e.g., turnover and the reproduction of capital) which Marx labels the 'sphere of circulation'; and Volume III is to elaborate upon a 'synthesis' (Marx actually uses this word) of the analyses of the first two volumes in order to reproduce the actual day-to-day workings of the complex economic system, as it appears to the actors in it, but now fully explained in terms of its components.

Thesis—antithesis—synthesis: these three words have been invoked as a charm by both admirers and despisers of dialectics since Kant, as a supposed means of getting at the heart of its meaning. Kant had invoked the terminology of thesis and antithesis by way of showing the impossibility of conclusively proving, despite reason's intense interest in doing so, either side of several pairs of contradictory claims concerning ultimate metaphysical issues— infinity and finitude, pluralism and monism, universal causality and freedom, the existence of a necessary being. The basic philosophical point of the subsequent movement of German idealism was to show that syntheses in such matters, and hence speculative philosophy, were possible after all. But Hegel, unlike some of his contemporaries, very seldom invokes the rigid terminology of 'thesis—antithesis—synthesis', and yet manages to remain a dialectician. Marx employs this terminology even less. This has led some sympathetic critics to maintain, in the case of Hegel and *a fortiori* in the case of Marx, that triadicity is not an important element of dialectical method. But to say this is to go too far.

True, the number three was often considered sacred and mystical in primitive thought, and the Christian doctrine of the Trinity was one of the early focal points of attack by religious and anti-religious rationalists alike during the Enlightenment. It is true as well that an unsympathetic reader of Hegel's writings is likely to find considerable comedy in his almost constant efforts to develop his presentations in the forms of triads and sub-triads and sub-subtriads. It is also true that we cannot consistently insist too strictly on the triadic structure of *Capital* itself: in Volume I, for instance, Marx very explicitly and dramatically announces a move from the sphere of circulation (supposedly the subject-matter of Volume II) to the sphere of production at the end of Chapter VI. Nevertheless, none of these considerations should stand in the way of the dialectician's contending that triadic rhythms abound in the ways in which we think and, consequently, act.

This apparently arcane and abstract claim can be substantiated in several ways, all of which are crucial to understanding the dialectical character of Marx's philosophical method. Thinking advances by way of negating; thinking advances by establishing a position between excessive generalization and excessive specificity; thinking advances by resolving the gross dissimilarity between the way in which we are convinced that things actually do function essentially, and the way in which they appear to function when we attend to their endless complexities. Prior to thinking at all about any given subject matter, there is confusion—a stage of innocence, ignorance, or, in Hegelian jargon, 'sheer immediacy'. This pre-cognitive stage is, by definition, not a part of any thought-process at all, and may for the moment be disregarded, though the avoidance of philosophical idealism rests on our acknowledgement of the historical existence of such a stage, both in the lives of individuals and in the development of societies.

In beginning actually to try to understand and explain any subject-matter, we first name it and identify it by what we take to be its most salient characteristic or characteristics. At this first stage, we are inclined to be sweeping and unspecific in our understanding. There may be a breathtaking simplicity and wholeness about our generalizations, but that is because they are based on comparative ignorance of details and disregard of complexities. Nevertheless, if we have been honest and diligent in formulating this first account of the subject-matter in question, we will be unlikely, according to the dialectician, completely to have missed the mark; even when we eventually come to reject the first formulation as wholly inadequate, we shall continue to recognize that there was some rough, basic truth to it.

A second stage of thinking can now be contrasted with this first one. Barring arrested development, we plunge into the subject-matter at hand in the effort to master it. New conceptions of the subject-matter arise by denying that the original conceptions were adequate or, consequently, entirely true. Negation thus enters into the thought process. At the same time, we revolt against the easy, insufficiently reflective generalizations of the first stage; we embark on a process of discovering specific details within our subject-matter. We analyse, in the literal sense of the word; that is, we cut our subject-matter apart (in thought) into small pieces. And we often discover, as the examples of the crude early atomists of Marx's Doctoral dissertation and of modern theoretical physicists both illustrate, that the 'particles' to which our analysis has led us are fundamentally different in kind from the original subject-matter, considered as a totality, that we had set out to explain. At the worst, we become lost in the mass of specifics or particulars that we have uncovered, and give up entirely on the attempt at explanation.

But a third stage is possible, and the understanding and explanation of any subject-matter depends on it. We now formulate the crucial judgement that merely to list a mass of details does not constitute a complete account, and in fact distorts the subject-matter; thus the previous rejection of the original generalization is now followed by a second, equally fundamental, denial—a denial that the bundle of details is the final word about the subject-matter. This new negation signifies, in one sense, a return in the direction of the original (first) stage, in as much as we now recognize that some generalization concerning our subject-matter is required, after all; however, the new generalization will not be sweeping and unspecific, as was the first, but will rather be tempered by incorporating and accounting for all the true facts that were discovered in the second stage. If we have been successful in this process, we shall be able to recognize that the individuals (persons or other entities) in our subject-matter are both general and specific at once—that is, characterized by certain shared, 'essential' qualities and yet also unique and separate from one another. And this is what is meant by 'explanation' or 'comprehension' of a subject-matter.

If the above appears, as I believe it should, to be a more or less common and recognizable thought-pattern, then we have made progress towards de-mystifying the method of dialectics, including its aspect of triadicity. Hegel and others have conferred various technical names on the three stages, depending in part on the contexts within which they appear in their writings. One of the most popular technical designations, which at least strikes one as considerably superior to 'thesis—antithesis—synthesis', is 'universal—particular—individual'. ('Concrete universal' and, less plausibly, 'singular' are sometimes used as substitute-terms for 'individual'.) Marx flirted with this terminology, though not to very great effect, in the large mass of unpublished notes towards an early version of *Capital* that now goes by the name of *Grundrisse*. Another important way of designating the second stage is to call it the stage of negation, with the third stage thus constituting the negation of the negation. Dialectical jargon also makes much use of the word 'contradiction', to designate the radical discrepancy between, in particular, the first and second stages; this misleads philosophers especially, since the same word has a quite different, rather more precise, meaning in Aristotelean and modern formal logic. Technicalities aside, the movement from broad generalizations to endless specifics to generalities qualified by facts is an extremely common one, discernible in the histories of intellectual disciplines and of popular cultural attitudes as well as in the development of individuals from the early stages of childhood.

The dialectician, like most philosophers, proceeds on the assumption that his or her understanding of the world is not fundamentally at odds with the way the world is. A dialectical view of the world, then, is one that stresses the systematic interrelatedness of entities within ever-developing larger wholes, or totalities, the structure of which is in principle comprehensible. Comprehension, for the dialectician, depends upon viewing the process of interaction among entities as involving opposition (negation, contradiction) that may ultimately lead not to stagnation or stalemate (though this is one possible result), but to positive outcomes in the form of more adequate entities. This process, whereby the very limitations inherent in initial stages are seen to lead to later stages through an internal dynamism, is called 'mediation': the entities in the earlier stages are the means, or instruments, by which the later stages are generated without external intervention. The later stages, which can be termed 'higher' in the sense of being more fully developed, though not necessarily in the sense of being morally better, will both incorporate features of the earlier and yet exhibit novel forms of their own. This is the meaning of the key German dialectical term '*Aufhebung*', 'surpassing' or 'transcending', which connotates at once both suppression and preservation. Within the totalistic and process-orientated conception of reality that is made possible by the dialectical method, and that receives confirmation from the sorts of commonplace experience to which I have alluded, these superficially contradictory connotations are reconciled.

If I have been correct, then it is an absurd exhibition of sheer prejudice to dismiss dialectical methodology out of hand as being simply mystifying and insupportable by evidence. To the extent to which Marx employs that method, he is simply using a basic tool of the human mind. And to the extent to which, rejecting (at least for the sake of hypothesis) dualism and idealism along with Marx, one accepts the view that the human mind is a part of material reality and in some way reflects it, the proper employment of that method guarantees one's arriving at some portion of truth about the world. Beyond these initial responses to totally hostile critics of Marx's method, however, there lie some genuinely serious difficulties, all of them at least partially unresolved by Marx himself. They have to do with (a) the extreme generality of the dialectical schema itself; (b) the relationship between the dialectical laws that Marx claims to have discovered and the real entities that these laws are supposed to govern; and (c) Marx's use of dialectics more as a tool of structural than of genetic analysis.

(a) It is not surprising that neither Hegel nor Marx ever wrote an account of more than a few paragraphs in length on the subject of the dialectical method as such. It is much easier to exhibit its use in specific sequences of ideas than to write about it in general. When Hegel did attempt to write about it in general, in the passage cited near the beginning of this chapter, he was more rhapsodic than informative. The trouble with the schema that I have provided, or with any similar schema, is that it must be expressed in terms sufficiently general to cover an extremely wide range of instances. Not only do instances differ greatly one from another, but the instances themselves also differ in degree of generality. In Hegel's philosophy, for example, the dialectical development of the consciousness of the slave or 'bondsman', which can be shown to fit my general schema, is intended to be and is in fact repeatable—in one way and another applicable to many human beings in many circumstances—whereas the major developments traced in his *Philosophy of History* (e.g., the decline of Classical Greece as epitomized in the person of Socrates, an especially suggestive Hegelian passage) are admittedly not. The methodology required to cope with these two kinds of sequences must itself differ somewhat, even if it also has much in common in the two cases. To begin to specify what the differences will be entails, of course, actually beginning to analyse the individual cases dialectically, rather than discussing dialectical method as such any longer.

To the extent to which this difficulty were to appear increasingly insurmountable, the method as applied to particular sequences would be seen increasingly to share common characteristics with other methods, whatever they might be. Techniques alleged to be uniquely dialectical would appear not to be uniquely so. Dialectical method would not so much be disproved (one does not prove or disprove a method, though one may show it to be more or less productive of results), as it would vanish. But such an outcome would not, in fact, leave the rest of Hegelianism or of Marxism just 'the way it was'; the entire philosophy of Marx is pervaded with dialectical turns of thought. Therefore, we must rest content with taking schematic and excessively general stabs at saying what the dialectical method is, without hoping ever to be able to draw neat lines around it. For, as a method, it is merely a tool for analysing reality, rather than a series of dogmatic propositions about the nature of reality.

(b) To say this, however, confronts us immediately with a more serious problem, one concerning the exact relationship between Marx's method and the subject-matters that he treats. For both Hegel and Marx believed, as I have noted, that in some sense reality is dialectical, in addition to dialectic's being a preferred method of thinking. In Hegel's case, the congruence between thought and reality was ensured by the postulate of idealism: if ideas (and finally the Idea) are ultimate reality, then to say that reality, as well as thinking, is dialectical becomes a redundancy. But Marx, as a materialist, boasts of no such built-in conceptual guarantee of congruence, transcending the actual data with which he has to work. He claimed that his own dialectic method was the 'direct opposite' of Hegel's; although this claim has no literal meaning (methods cannot have opposites any more than they can be strictly proved or disproved, it makes some sense as a reference to the divergence between Marx's materialist postulates and Hegel's idealism. The former, which we shall consider in detail in the next chapter, amount to the assumptions that human thought and activity are parts of a larger material universe and that the most important causal determinants of human thought and activity are to be found outside of these phenomena themselves, in that larger universe. At present, we are concerned with the implications of these postulates for Marx's dialectical method rather than with problems inherent in the postulates. The minimal implication, it seems clear, is that the assertion that reality is dialectical must mean something quite different for Marx from what it means for Hegel.

If the causal determination of human thought by other factors in the material universe (e.g., the development of a full-blown materialist philosophy of history as a result of an increase in the abundance of material resources) were such that thought automatically registered the existence and nature of all such factors, then there would be no such things as philosophical difficulties: all would be transparent. However, this is not the case, and Marx himself lays the greatest stress both on the practical impossibility of anyone's having achieved the most important theoretical breakthroughs that he has achieved in any epoch prior to his own, and on the amount of effort that has been required even for him to achieve them. Marx claims to have *discovered* certain 'laws' of the natural history of human society, or at least (if we consider the more modest claims that he makes in his correspondence) of a segment of human society, that of so-called modern Western civilization. These laws are, presumably, nothing but accurate high-level generalizations concerning a wide range of phenomena (although, to be candid, the failure to say very much about the meaning of the term 'law' as he uses it is one of the most gaping lacunae in Marx's all too brief discussions of methodology). If one accepts the postulates of Marx's materialism, one must assume that some of the underlying causal factors which determine human society to be what it is were also at work in determining Marx's own thought processes—both the lengthy preliminary processes of inquiry and the processes whereby he presented his results in dialectical form. But these results, the 'dialectical laws' of society, are themselves thought products; they will, if Marx has been successful (i.e., well or properly determined), reflect or reproduce the underlying causal factors, but they cannot themselves *be* such factors.

Consequently, the reviewer's claim about Marx's findings concerning 'the social movement' (namely, that it is 'governed by laws not only independent of human will, consciousness, and intelligence, but rather, on the contrary, determining that will, consciousness, and intelligence') must be rejected as misleading within the philosophy of Marx, even in the face of Marx's seeming endorsement of it. The laws in question cannot be what determine thought, for the laws, the dialectical generalizations discovered and formulated by Marx, have no such causal efficacy. (The publication of them may subsequently have exerted, and may continue to exert, some causal influence on Marx's readers, but that is another matter.) To say that they do is to regress into idealism.

What implications does this have for Marx's method? We must take very seriously his own emphasis (which goes well beyond an apparent endorsement of his reviewer's words) on the distinction between the method of presentation, which he fears may seem ideal because too perfect a reflection of the subject-matter, and the method of inquiry which preceded it. The latter may well have been determined by causal factors that are themselves ultimately describable in dialectical laws, but just how this was the case cannot have been apparent to the inquirer (Marx) at the time of his inquiry, or else the whole process could have been expedited considerably. The method of inquiry is a descriptive (phenomenological, though not in Hegel's technical sense of this word) method. It was structured and guided by Marx with increasing care as his inquiry went on over the years, but it is certainly not obviously 'dialectical' in the sense of fitting neatly within a progressive, synthetic triadic schematism. The method of presentation, particularly as it is employed in *Capital,* on the other hand, is the dialectical method proper. It is held to be the key to providing an accurate reproduction of reality, beyond the capacities of rival methods. And so it may be, but there is no way of supporting this claim other than by constantly checking the 'presentation' itself, the theoretical text, against the raw data that it is supposed to explain.

The dialectical method, thus understood, could have been applied by Marx to any of a vast range of subject-matters. Whether Marx would have met with the same success if he had applied it in detail to subject-matters with which he did not in fact greatly concern himself, such as the natural sciences, is a question that cannot be decided in advance since Marxism provides no transcendental guarantee of the all-pervasiveness of dialectical patterning. (This manner of stating the case, by the way, helps undercut the great recent dispute among Continental Marxists over the theoretical justifiability of Engels's conception of a dialectics of nature. To say, against Engels, that only human beings function dialectically, whereas non-human nature does not and cannot, is to espouse a metaphysical dualism, incompatible with the materialist postulates of Marx; to maintain, on the other side, that the philosophy of Marx would be falsified if dialectical laws were not found to prevail in all domains of natural phenomena is to make *a priori* claims about the nature of the universe for which Marxism, in opposition to the assertions of Hegelianism, provides no warrant.)

At any rate, the subject-matter upon which Marx chose largely to concentrate, for reasons discussed in Chapter 1, was the subject-matter of political economy. He was most concerned with the workings of the economic system, including the groups—the social classes—that played major roles, as groups, within capitalism, and he found the dialectical method useful in accounting for their interactions. To put it simply, Marx presented the bourgeois class, with its emphasis on the supremacy of private property rights by contrast with the hierarchical but communally oriented feudal system, as having replaced that universalistic system by one in which particularity dominated; but he saw the very development of modern capitalism, in the direction of increasingly efficient exploitation of its working class for the sake of ever greater capital accumulation, as generating its own internal opposition in the form of a cohesive workers' movement, the self-interest of which dictated the abolition of the regime of extreme particularity. This is a very plausible, eminently dialectical presentation, as far as class relationships are concerned.

But what of the individual human beings who constitute groups —would the dialectical method also be useful in explaining the ways in which socio-economic factors influence the development of their personal thought-patterns and activities? One would certainly expect Marx to maintain that it would, but, unfortunately, he has very little to say about this. In a famous passage in the Preface to his first edition of *Capital,* he defends himself against the anticipated criticism that he has been insufficiently moralistic in his treatment of capitalists and landlords. 'Here', he points out, 'individuals are dealt with only in so far as they are the personifications of economic categories, embodiments of particular class-relations and class-interests' (*Capital,* Vol. I, Preface). This is well and good, both as a justification for Marx's general refusal to emphasize moral categories in his analyses and as an effort to establish parameters around his subject-matter in *Capital,* but it cannot be construed as an outright denial of the possibility of dealing dialectically, within a Marxian framework, with the development of individuals as individuals. It would be nonsense to claim that capitalists are personifications *and nothing more*; they must actively play their capitalistic roles in order for the system to continue to operate, even though Marx is undoubtedly correct in emphasizing the extent to which they are driven to play these roles by practical necessities, rather than freely choosing them.

In fact, it is of great theoretical importance for the philosophy of Marx to be able to account, for instance, for the possibility of a few individuals advocating the revolutionary expropriation of the means of production in a period of general acquiescence in the established order of things, or for the phenomenon of ideological mystification (e.g., the mentality of the anti-Marxist worker, who presumably fails to be aware of what is in his own interest); it is likewise important to explain how a son of the nineteenth-century bourgeoisie, born in a sleepy city in the Rhineland, could have discovered and formulated certain fundamental 'laws of motion' of modern society. Given the human mind's propensity, as I have sketched it, to pursue broadly dialectical patterns, one would expect the dialectical method to be of great assistance in such matters. But Marx himself, while readily acknowledging the existence of such phenomena as the rise or retardation of class-consciousness and individuals identifying themselves with the interests of classes opposed to their own, seldom provides us with detailed dialectical analyses of their occurrence.

Had he done so—that is, had he shown more frequently (as he occasionally does, particularly in his historical writings) how 'human will, consciousness, and intelligence' themselves functioned dialectically in specific instances or situations—he would have considerably strengthened his claims concerning the superiority of his method. But it would still have remained the case that, unlike the idealist who begins by assuming that thought is what is ultimately real, the Marxist is entitled to say that reality is dialectical only if, and to the extent to which, the areas of reality which he or she has analysed seem best explained or 'reflected' in a dialectical presentation of them.

(c) We have seen that Marx's dialectical account of capitalism does not pretend to reproduce the historical 'method of inquiry' of Marx himself (i.e., the actual progression of the inquiry in the course of his own life-history); in addition, it does not pretend to reproduce the historical development of capitalism, either. The issue concerning the relationship between the sequence of categories and the actual sequence of history is a very complicated one as far as Hegel's *Phenomenology* and *Philosophy of Right* are concerned, but at any rate there is no doubt that Hegel relied heavily on the sweep of Western history, as structured in his *Philosophy of History*, to help vindicate the superiority of dialectics and validate the claim that reality was dialectical. Marx too, as we have noted, clearly had a general vision of history as following a dialectical progression; in both his early and later writings, he thinks of the period of capitalism as one of 'negation'—on the whole an advance over feudalism, surely necessary to make a later transition to socialism possible, and yet characterized by an increase in the atomization of human beings and interest groups—and of a future communist or socialist society as being, at least in its initial stages, 'negation of the negation'. But the dialectical argument of *Capital* itself and of Marx's other economic writings is explicitly ahistorical.

In a complicated essay on 'The Method of Political Economy', intended to serve as one part of the Introduction to the *Grundrisse*, Marx reasons, in effect, that there are two types of abstract concepts with which one can begin analysing the socio-economic sphere: seemingly concrete but in fact empty and scientifically worthless global generalizations such as 'population', and terms that may appear to be more abstract but are in fact capable of being assigned precise and evolving meanings for different periods of history, such as 'labour'. It is appropriate, says Marx, to begin with abstractions of the latter sort (as indeed he later did in *Capital*) and to proceed to describe systematically and in detail the precise forms that they have taken on in the present period, until a fully concrete, structured account of modern society emerges. The requisite level of abstraction or generalization may not have become attainable, intellectually speaking, until the modern era of history—witness the provincial narrowness of Aristotle's conception of labour as primarily slave labour, for instance—but this does not mean that the proper dialectical method consists in reproducing, step by step, the historical development of the concept and the phenomena to which it corresponds; quite the contrary. 'Human anatomy contains a key to the anatomy of the ape', rather than *vice versa*. In other words, an all-sided, complete understanding even of primitive forms of a particular sort of entity first becomes possible only when we can study the most complex, highly developed form.

Although Marx did not include a similar methodological explanation in *Capital*, perhaps in part because the distinction between the 'good' and 'bad' sorts of abstraction is an elusive one, he continued to follow the guidelines set out in his earlier essay. His brief account of the expropriation of the English feudal yeomanry, for instance, in which he summarizes his views concerning the genesis of the present capitalist system, does not occur until the final section of Volume I; the detailed study of (monetary) interest as an important but subsidiary element of the system as a whole is relegated to a late section of Volume III, even though Marx is perfectly aware of the fact that the rise of banking in the late Middle

Ages was one of the earliest historical manifestations of the nascent new economic order.

It is therefore correct to characterize Marx's dialectical approach in his most central later writing (though not in all of his writings) as being a structural, rather than a genetic or historical, one. Capitalism can only be understood, he believes, through a dialectical examination (sphere of production—sphere of circulation—process of capitalist production as a whole) of it in its most fully developed form. Is that form simply the England of Marx's day, as some commentators who would like to regard *Capital* as primarily a history book have attempted to maintain? Not quite. True, Marx uses primarily English data in the more empirical parts of his work, because he clearly regards England as the most advanced capitalist country of his day—a rather uncontroversial position. But the capitalist system that constitutes the object of Marx's dialectical analysis is not identical with the historical England of 1867 or any other year, as the following sentence in an obscure footnote makes evident:

In order to examine the object of our investigation in its integrity, free from all disturbing subsidiary circumstances, we must treat the whole world as one nation, and assume that capitalist production is everywhere established and has possessed itself of every branch of industry. (*Capital*, Vol. I, Chap. XXIV, Section 1.)

There is nothing inherently wrong with this ideal-typical approach, which every theorist is forced to use to some extent if he or she wishes to be able to achieve a sufficiently high level of generalization to be interesting. But it does raise some difficult questions for the philosophy of Marx.

The citation implies that no stage of the historical socio-economic system known as capitalism either did, does, or presumably (although this is somewhat more controversial and ambiguous) ever will correspond *exactly* with the idealization of it set forth in Marx's writings. (The same has frequently been said, by Marx among others, about the so-called 'system of perfect competition' idealized by apologists of capitalism.) Marx was most insistent, as a good dialectician, on the dynamism of the system—its tendency to evolve constantly, in significant ways. Nevertheless, what he has analysed for us most systematically and in greatest detail is a definite, determinate structure, albeit a dynamic structure, that presumably corresponds closely but not exactly to the most salient features discernible (along with the most salient future trends that he could project) in an actual historical society, mid-nineteenth-century England. That society still happens to be quite close in time and form to the one in which I myself live (although some features, such as the relative prominence of joint-stock companies and the comparative role of monopolies, have changed significantly), so that it does not surprise me to find that Marx's method aids me in understanding my own society as well as his.

But can there be any guarantee in principle that the method will always be similarly helpful in the future? Once again here, as in the case of our previous considerations, Marx's materialism precludes his appealing to an alleged transcendental entity to provide such a guarantee. Marx anticipated the imminent collapse of the capitalist system and its replacement by another kind; but what if this expectation is both partially met and partially frustrated, so that what ensues is neither a neat replacement of the old structure by a radically new one nor a simple continuation of the old structure in its main features? The Marxist can hope that the structural dialectical method that I have been outlining will still be more useful than any other in explaining the new state of affairs—he or she may even be confident that it will be—but it is impossible to prove in advance that it will be.

Now let us suppose the occurrence of the alternative possibility, the one actually expected by Marx—namely, a worldwide fundamental change from capitalism to a new form of society, a 'society of associated producers'. In this event, difficulties emerge both concerning the use of the dialectical method to analyse historical developments and its use as a tool of structural analysis. Let us admit that there is a certain rough plausibility about seeing the projected next stage of Western society as 'negation of the negation', with feudalism occupying the first, and capitalism the second, position in this triad. (A post-capitalist society of the sort envisaged by Marx would eliminate the particularity of capitalist private ownership while preserving and strengthening individuality in other ways. The progression thus described replicates the general schema of dialectics upon which I have elaborated.) But history, even Western history, is not reducible to just three principal 'moments' or stages; to begin with, there were, as Marx shows very well in his work on pre-capitalist economic formations, other interestingly different formations preceding feudalism. And is history, conceived of as a dialectical progression of stages characterized by radically different

C

social structures, supposed to come to an end with the coming of a society of associated producers?

Some of Marx's critics think that this was his view, and there is at least one sentence in one of his *1844 Manuscripts*, Heraclitean in its obscurity ('[Communism] is the riddle of history solved and knows itself as this solution'), that lends itself to this interpretation. At the very end of this same manuscript, however, Marx clearly states that communism as such is not 'the goal of human development', but rather a necessary next phase on the road towards human emancipation, and elsewhere he insists that history, far from ending with the abolition of capitalism, will only begin in its fullest sense at that time. Whatever this claim may mean, it certainly puts into question the notion that the dialectical method will no longer be useful for the analysis of history after capitalism's projected demise, or that, as far as Marx is concerned, reality will in some magical way cease to follow dialectical patterns at that time. *Change*, at least, will continue to occur, and the dialectical method is peculiarly suited to analyse change.

There is, then, some difficulty, though perhaps not an insurmountable one, in admitting, within the conceptual framework of Marx's thought, the applicability of a dialectical analysis of *historical* developments in a definitively post-capitalist society; it is this difficulty that has led to greatly exaggerated charges, by some critics, to the effect that Marx conceives of the future eschatologically—that is, as a secular substitute for theology's Beatific Vision. But there is an even greater difficulty, given what Marx had to say about the fullness of the evolution of such basic socio-economic categories as 'labour' under modern capitalism, in conceiving of a dialectical analysis of the *structure* of post-capitalist society that would be comparable to *Capital*. Would this structure be a dialectical, or a dialectically analysable, one? Would it be characterized by practical 'contradictions' of the sort that Marx, profiting from his proficiency in the use of dialectical techniques, delighted in pointing up within the capitalist structure? In particular, would there be some sort of deep discrepancy, of the sort epitomized in the dramatic contrast between the sphere of circulation and the sphere of production in *Capital*, between social appearances and the socio-economic 'essence' of a future society of associated producers? (Mao Tse-tung's distinction between non-antagonistic contradictions, which would still obtain in a post-capitalist society, and antagonistic ones, which would not, is a primarily verbal solution, but it has the merit of recognizing the seriousness of this philosophical problem.)

Marx says next to nothing about these issues, in large measure because, for reasons to be considered in Chapters 6 and 7, he generally eschews discussions of a post-capitalist society. But I am hard put to see how a harmonious, fully developed socialist society (as distinct from one in the process of development) having the numerous characteristics that Marx attributes, in the scattered passages that serve as exceptions to his general rule of non-discussion, to such a society, could possibly be subject to a dialectical analysis comparable to that contained in *Capital*. For a dialectical analysis of the *structural* sort to work, one needs basic (not simply superficial) oppositions within the structure; but the envisaged society of associated producers is one in which, by definition, such oppositions have been overcome. Realistically speaking, most of us have the intuition that there will never be such a time in human history: at best, we may be inclined to concede, fundamental antagonisms might cease to be of the socio-economic sort that Marx discerned in capitalism and might become primarily non-economic. All such discussions quickly become highly speculative and reflective of the limitations of our imaginations. But let us just suppose a society in which no fundamental antagonisms of any variety existed, so that a dialectical analysis of such a society had been rendered impossible; what does the conception of such a state of affairs do to our estimation of Marx's dialectical method?

Very little, if my interpretation of it is accepted. For the value of such a method, given Marx's rejection of the idealist thesis that thought is the ultimate reality, can only be vindicated by checking the results obtained through its use against the perceived empirical data. If, as I have been contending, Marx's philosophy leaves no room for any transcendental guarantor that all reality is, always has been, and always will be inherently dialectical (whatever meaning such a claim might be made to have), then there is neither a possibility nor a need of 'proving' that the dialectical method is in all circumstances superior to every other method in philosophy and science, and one is justified in taking a more relaxed attitude towards its employment than the fierce polemics which continue to surround it may have led one to think.

The usefulness of the dialectical method in analysing present-day society, at any rate, seems to me perfectly obvious. As I have mentioned, Marx ended his brief methodological remarks in the

Afterword to the second German edition of *Capital* by pointing to the value of dialectic as a tool of radical criticism:

> In its rational form [dialectic] is a scandal and abomination to bourgeoisdom and its doctrinaire professors, because it includes in its comprehension and affirmative recognition of the existing state of things, at the same time also, the recognition of the negation of that state, of its inevitable breaking up; because it regards every historically developed social form as in fluid movement, and therefore takes into account its transient nature not less than its momentary existence; because it lets nothing impose upon it, and is in its essence critical and revolutionary. (*Capital*, Vol. I, Afterword to the second German edition.)

The adjective 'critical' here must be understood as redolent of the connotations of the Kantian word *Kritik*: a rigorous, detailed internal analysis, leading in the end to a finding of necessary inadequacy or incompleteness—but only at the end. Marx's purpose in writing much of what he did was, for reasons discussed in Chapter 1, one of emphasizing the possibilities for radically changing everyday social life; the dialectical method was a most suitable intellectual tool for accomplishing this purpose.

Of all the kinds of practical 'contradictions' that Marx detects in his society, surely the most pervasive is that between, to use a traditional philosophical terminology, appearance and essence. ('Essence' is not an ideal choice of word, since it means something different, something more metaphysical, in the writings of both Hegel and Aristotle, than it does in its very occasional employment by Marx. Marx is not referring to allegedly eternal essences, but rather to underlying mechanisms, detectable only after lengthy analysis, within an existing system—in particular, within the capitalist system that most interests him. Still, no alternative choice of word conveys the idea much better. When referring to the 'appearances' of some aspect of a social system, Marx often uses the word 'forms'.)

The principal drama of the early pages of *Capital* consists in showing the vast discrepancy between the superficial level of appearances, the 'sphere of simple circulation or of exchange of commodities', at which workers and employees in modern society operate as legal equals, and the 'essential' sphere of production, where matters are quite different. From the perspective of the former sphere, freedom of contract prevails for both classes, the one deriving wages and the other profits from the outcome of work contracts. Within the sphere of production, on the other hand, relationships of dominance and subordination prevail, thus rendering hollow the slogans of equality and freedom. Since Marx is no idealist, the surface sphere of appearances is no *mere* illusion for him: the worker is at one and the same time free in terms of one set of categories and unfree in terms of another. The complicated interplay of these categories in the actual lives of the system's different actors is made to account for the total, seemingly confused reality that is the socio-economic world of Marx's time; Marx attempts to sort out and explain the salient confusions without simply defining them out of existence.

There are moments when he has great success in doing this. These are the moments when the dialectical method, with its emphasis on comprehensiveness of analysis, on the existence of internal tensions or 'contradictions', and on the possibility of radical change, shows up to best advantage.

4 Descriptive Generalization I: Materialist Metaphysics

In pursuing his ultimate aim of delineating social conditions with a view to pointing to the possibilities for fundamental change, Marx made a number of declarative statements that, unlike his mere espousal of the dialectical method, involve claims about the way things are. These claims form the core of his philosophy, and indeed of his entire theory—although, to be sure, his method is a scarcely dispensable tool in enabling him to make them, and although they are fully understandable only in light of what I call Marx's vision of a possible future. The range of generalization to be found among these claims is enormous, extending from interpretations of historical details to cosmic overviews. Even the former are often of some philosophical interest, since the meaning of Marx's more basic interpretative categories is frequently clarified by his employment of them in specific instances. But philosophers tend, as it were constitutionally, to be more interested in the more general, and it is therefore upon this that we shall concentrate here.

For purposes of convenience, though not with a view to establishing a rigid dividing-line, I propose to distinguish between the most general of Marxian generalizations—i.e., those that most closely approach the cosmic—and generalizations having to do with history and with particular societies, notably Western capitalist society. Generalizations of the former sort, which can be called 'metaphysical' in a loose sense (the sense that they include concepts frequently dealt with in philosophy courses on metaphysics), will occupy the present chapter, and those of the latter sort will occupy the next. I shall then devote a separate chapter to a third type of generalization that is frequently attributed to Marx—namely, future predictions—since these involve quite separate and peculiar problems.

Implicit in this way of ordering our subject-matter is a certain somewhat controversial view of the nature of broad philosophical claims. I take them to be attempts, more ambitious than those ordinarily made even by general theorists in other disciplines, to describe or characterize large swathes of reality, and sometimes all reality. As such, even idealist generalizations about 'the Absolute' are meaningful, even if ill-founded and wrong. But such claims, in my view, are radically different only in scope, and not in kind, from relatively more modest generalizations about, let us say, the nature of capitalism; and no drastically different sort of knowing is involved in them. Thus, the newly popular expression 'descriptive metaphysics' is redundant, since all metaphysics in the loose sense in which the term is being used here (as distinguished from the technical sense of Marx and Engels in their criticism of the 'narrow, metaphysical mode of thinking') is descriptive, if it is anything. (On the other hand, since many traditional metaphysicians did not think of their enterprises in this way, the term may have some value as a way of contrasting newer with older approaches.) At any rate, whatever its other merits and weaknesses may be, I find this approach useful in undercutting some of the Continental controversies about whether or not classical Marxism includes a metaphysics or, to use the somewhat purer and less worn-out term, 'ontology'.

The task of reproducing Marx's explicit and implicit highest-level generalizations about the world is difficult for two reasons. First, as I have already noted in my discussion of Engels in Chapter 2, it was he, rather than Marx, who had a great penchant for cosmic utterances, and it is questionable whether some of his elegant simplifications of the Marxist categorical framework should properly be attributed to Marx himself, even when the latter let them pass with his apparent approval. We shall simply have to deal with this problem when and as it arises in our exposition. The second reason, of greater philosophical importance than the first, is that the philosophy of Marx contains, in its attack on all 'ideology', an element that is so destructive of systems of global generalizations and so strongly relativistic as to render very precarious any of its own broad claims about reality. We shall therefore have to consider this negative, or critical, aspect of Marx's 'metaphysics' before turning to its seemingly more positive assertions about the ultimacy of matter and about the place of humanity in this material universe.

The German Ideology is a joint, fairly early work of Marx and Engels. It was left uncompleted, and in its extant form it is cumbersome and ponderous. Moreover, it is surprisingly difficult to extract from any section of it a straightforward exposition of its supposedly central term, 'ideology', that is at all adequate in length or detail. Nevertheless, the authors' basic insight is comparatively easy to reconstruct. The word *idéologues*, first applied contemptuously by Napoleon to a group of French thinkers of his own era, retains its original pejorative connotation in the work of Marx and Engels, as it has not always done in the writings of some later Marxists. The Marxian account goes like this. Philosophers and other theorists have traditionally maintained that their conceptual systems are logically independent of the times and places in which they have been enunciated. The most forceful and sophisticated (since it does take history into account, even while pretending to transcend it) expression of this claim is to be found in Hegel's idealism, but even the generation of critical thinkers that has succeeded him has tended, on the whole, to consider ideas to be the driving forces of human history, and hence to regard their thought-revolutions as the most important events in contemporary German society. But neither anthropological and historical evidence nor our common-sense intuitions, when we attempt imaginatively to reconstruct the development of the human race, support the attribution of priority, whether temporal or logical, to ideas over the material conditions of life in explaining what has happened; on the contrary. Moreover, the roles of various past philosophies in advancing the interests of particular social sub-groups with which the individual philosophers in question have been associated can easily be pinpointed and documented. In the majority of cases, in the history of Western philosophy, philosophers' systems have served to justify the continued dominance of their societies' most powerful group or groups, if not with blatant explicitness, then at least by containing epistemologies and ontologies that have fitted well with the predominant self-images of the groups' members. In other cases, philosophical systems have expressed, in complex and esoterical forms, the interests either of once dominant but declining groups (the phenomenon of reactionary ideologies) or of groups coming to ascendancy (as in the cases of Enlightenment philosophies favourable to the rising bourgeoisie). Since large social classes and other social groups are seldom homogeneous, particularly in modern times, and since the great philosophers of the past have never, on the basis of the evidence, been entirely clear concerning the ideological roles that their systems were destined to play, we should be careful not to expect correspondences between ideologies and social groups always to be either simple and direct or instantaneously discoverable.

This, in a nutshell, is the Marxian conception of ideology, particularly as it applies to philosophical systems. Marx and Engels intend other types of conceptual frameworks to fall under the general rubric of 'ideology' as well; at one point, they speak of 'morality, religion, metaphysics, and all the rest of ideology and their corresponding forms of consciousness'. (I take 'morality' here to refer to moral philosophies and other sorts of ethical systems.) Implicit in this list is that thought-frameworks of quite varied degrees of sophistication, from the highly esoteric to the common-place, can exert similar functions in fixing the mind-sets of large groups of people, buttressing them against change.

The principal importance of this theory of ideology, as I see it, lies in its heuristic value as a tool of criticism of philosophies and other types of theories and thought-frameworks. It can be devastating. No part of traditional philosophy, with the possible exception of the purely syntactical elements of formal logic, is totally immune to it. It is the culmination of the Kantian critical tradition of philosophy undermining its own pretensions. And it has itself had a profound historical effect, even on many who are unaware of its point of origin.

Many of the more positive or constructive claims that have often been assumed to be implied by this Marxian theory, on the other hand, quickly run aground when subjected to close scrutiny. For instance, one might expect to be able automatically to identify the group in the interests of which an ideological statement is being made, on the basis of some definite, simple, and limited combination of facts about the ideologist, such as the social class into which he was born; but such, as we know even from the counter-examples of Marx and Engels themselves (who, by their own account, emancipated themselves from the ideology of the class into which they were born), is not always the case. And one might easily infer, from what is said in *The German Ideology*, an entire Marxist theory of thought as being mere epiphenomenon, generated (through layers of material and social reality that have to be designated by the excessively simplistic dichotomous pair 'base and superstructure') by non-cognitive material elements, but impotent to act upon those elements. But Engels, in his correspondence, took great pains to repudiate this interpretation, asserting that he and Marx had meant only to insist, against the strong idealist tide in the German culture of their early years, on the *ultimate* priority of material conditions over ideas in social causal explanation, and nothing more; he feared that they themselves in their zeal to combat idealism had been partly to blame for the epiphenomenalist (my word) misinterpretation of their philosophy by some of their followers, and acknowledged that ideas, once generated, could and did indeed sometimes exert a reciprocal influence on material conditions. In this case, although the letters in question are written after Marx's death, I take Engels to be expressing a point of view that, as far as I have reproduced it here, is consistent with the philosophy of Marx and in particular with the search for mutual interactions which is a hallmark of the dialectical method. If this is true, however, it once again (happily, in my opinion) renders the positive side of the Marxian theory of ideology irreducible to a few simple, easily refutable propositions about a supposed one-to-one correspondence between elements in the material 'base' and elements in the social 'superstructure', with all cause-and-effect relationships occurring unidirectionally from the former to the latter.

The value of the theory of ideology, then, it should be repeated, is primarily that of a heuristic, critical tool, not that of the first tenet of an allegedly infallible creed; as such, it seems to me, its importance for philosophy and for social thought in general is actually greater. One question remains to be considered concerning that theory, and it is probably the most obvious and nagging of all: if all previous philosophies and social theories can be demonstrated to have been ideological, then what is Marxism? For, presumably, Marx and Engels would like their own work to be regarded as escaping from the negative judgement that is implicit in the label of 'ideology' as they use it.

Several diverse answers, not entirely incompatible with one another, can be given. First, of course, it can be said that Marxism rises above the level of the ideological systems of the past sheerly by virtue of having identified the phenomenon of ideology, and hence that level. Looking forward to the future, the Marxist can maintain that Marxism heralds the end of ideological thinking ('the end of ideology' and in particular 'the end of philosophy', both expressions that have been given diverse and controversial interpretations in this century) and a society in which 'positive', unmystified ways of thinking will prevail; this conception is reinforced by the idea of a classless society, since the divergence of particular group-interests which is held to be the basis of the phenomenon of ideology is regarded as essentially a divergence of *class*-interests. Engels carries this line of thinking so far as to write, in several places, that all that will remain of past philosophy (besides, presumably, its study as an historical curiosity, of antiquarian interest) will be logic and the laws of thought—i.e., dialectical laws. This brings him, in this respect, surprisingly close to a principal theme of the nineteenth-century 'positivism' of Auguste Comte and his intellectual heirs: both stress the death of traditional philosophy, which they associate with mystification, and the eventual triumph of 'positive', scientific thinking. In the meantime, however, ideological thought of all kinds continues to abound in our world; there should be no dispute on this point. Therefore, many contemporary Marxists have come to accept the label of 'ideology' as an historically provisional name for Marxism as well, since Marxism does identify itself with the interests of one particular class (the proletariat) among the several that currently exist, even while looking to a future classless society, and since Marxism must at present be opposed to alternative thought-systems on an ideological level, even while anticipating a future society whose members' thinking will no longer take place on that level.

Often academic debates about this issue become encumbered by a kind of linguistic fetishism, or Platonism: the antagonists begin to believe that there exist, independently of the ways in which we our-selves use the words, an essence of 'ideology', an essence of 'philosophy', an essence of 'science', and so on, and that it is their duty to determine precisely whether, and to what extent, Marxism and other thought-systems fit within the boundaries of these essences. But this is completely contrary to the spirit of Marx's philosophy. Once one has become convinced of the usefulness of Marx's theory of ideology as a critical tool, it matters relatively little whether or not one chooses to apply the label 'ideology' to the language in which Marx and others expound this theory. But a much more serious philosophical problem lies behind these debates: it is the problem of relativism.

Engels goes very far indeed along the relativist path. He lays against bourgeois ideology the charge of believing in the real and eternal existence of such abstract Absolutes as Truth, Reason, and Justice —the sort of terms to which Plato devoted so much of his attention. Engels places Marxism squarely behind the denial of such beliefs, and even subscribes, in one passage (in *The Housing Question*) on the subject of justice, to the view that the term means something different to each individual who uses it. Marx, as ever more cautious than his colleague, devotes very little attention to the explicit refutation of Absolutism (that is, the belief in Absolutes). His writings, including *Capital,* contain a handful of brief references to 'justice'—an especially good test-case because of its historical importance for political philosophy, its emotional impact, and its comparative lack of connotations of a univocal, empirically referrable sort—that define it to mean action in accordance with the established rules of the dominant socio-economic system, and nothing more. To this extent (relativity of meanings to particular systems, though not to particular members of the system), and with respect at least to this one concept 'justice', then, Marx seems to be in agreement with the philosophical relativism of Engels.

But even on this issue, ambiguities remain. Marx clearly anticipates an eventual language reform which would result in the elimination of the word 'justice' and similar abstractions from our vocabularies. His own writings, on the whole, exemplify the anticipated new language in this respect; that is, Marx seldom uses such words in contexts in which most past social and political theorists would have used them. However, he needed, logically speaking, to write from a standpoint not identical with that of any dominant past or present social system's conception of justice in order to be able to assert the historical relativity of all such conceptions, and in fact there is one crucial point (in Volume I of *Capital*) in which he characterizes the contract between capitalist and worker as being entirely just and equal from the capitalist standpoint, and yet at the same time unequal and 'a trick' from the critical standpoint that is his own. Does this standpoint constitute a rival Marxian conception of justice? Not exactly, unless the modern chemist can be said to have a modern conception, different from the old one, of phlogiston (the imaginary substance once thought to be released during combustion) —a term to which Engels draws some interesting but ultimately imperfect analogies with 'justice'. But there must at least be said to be a Marxian conception *about* justice, some general account of how the English word and its equivalents in many languages have been used ideologically throughout the ages. And the building-blocks of this account cannot themselves be relative strictly to each particular historical society, or else no account could be given.

(There are many close parallels between these reflections on the status of 'justice' in Marx's philosophy and similar considerations about the status of 'freedom'. The major difference, of course, is that even Marx, to say nothing of Engels, sometimes speaks glowingly of a 'realm of freedom' that lies 'beyond the sphere of material production'. To the claim of capitalist ideologues that 'freedom' is fully realized in the so-called 'free market', Marx is not content with answering simply that his opponents' notion of freedom, like all other notions of freedom, is valid only within the system of capitalism and totally meaningless outside it; rather, he holds that the actors in a 'free market' situation are at once wholly free in one limited sense and, whether capitalists, workers, or others, unfree in other senses.)

The 'building-blocks' to which I refer are obviously not eternal values of any sort, nor can they be some allegedly Necessary Being or Beings; Marx rejected all such notions for lack of evidence to support them. They are generalizations about the course of history, and about the behaviour of the major stages and types of society that have gone to make it up; such generalizations will be the subject-matter of the next chapter. And beyond that? In order—to continue with the example that I have been using—for Marx's explanation of justice as always having served an ideological function in history to make sense, must there not be some implicit trans-temporal Marxian conception of such traditional metaphysical concerns as Time, History itself, and Causality?

Trans-temporal, yes, but *not* transcendental. In other words, Marx broke completely, as even the historically minded Hegel had not, with the dominant, paradoxical belief of traditional Western philosophy (so heavily influenced by religious thought) that there exists some sort of timeless time *outside* the stream of historical time in which we live, and of which we have empirical evidence. Marx would have been very receptive, I think, to the now widespread interest among philosophers, psychologists, anthropologists, and others in the divergence of ways in which time is perceived among different social groups. Such data would have added to the sophistication of his generalizations about history, since the very concept of history always implies a passage of time. But Marx needed no metaphysical theory about 'Time-as-Such', or some such alleged entity, in order to make these generalizations.

I refer once more to Marx's previously mentioned denial, contained in his correspondence, that his was a historico-philosophical theory intended to be applicable to all times and societies, and hence in fact applicable to none. This strikes me as the most consistent position for him to take, although I have no doubt that passages can be found throughout his writing in which it would be arguable to maintain that he leans in the 'historico-philosophical' direction. On the whole, however, Marx is far from being the 'historicist', the pedlar of a transcendental theory about the whole of history, past and future, that Karl Popper and others have so unfairly charged him with being. Even the famous opening of *The Communist Manifesto*, a popularization of Marxism in which one might expect some hyperbole, generalizes only about 'the history of all *hitherto existing* society' [my emphasis]. The reason for this qualification is obvious: the point being made is that past history has been characterized by class struggle, and of course the anticipation of a classless society entails the anticipation of a future time without class struggle. But then Engels, who was usually far more of a transgressor of strictures against transcendental metaphysical pronouncements about the universe than Marx was, felt compelled to add a further qualifying footnote to later editions of the *Manifesto*, on the basis of certain anthropological findings by Morgan. Engels's footnote in effect limits the generalization to hitherto existing *post-primitive* societies. It makes no difference, for our immediate purposes, whether Morgan was right or wrong about primitive communism; Engels's action shows the extent to which even he, to say nothing of Marx, considered Marxism's generalizations about history to be based on empirical evidence rather than on an *a priori* metaphysical stance.

But must there not at least exist such a Marxian stance concerning the nature of causality? At any rate, no explicit general theory of causality is to be found in Marx's writings, although he makes many references to the influence of a society's material, economic foundation on its property relations and ideologies. The profound confusions about the workings of society that were to be found both in the philosophies (especially Hegel's) that he had studied in his university days and in most of the ('utopian') socialisms with which he had become acquainted during the following years were largely traceable, Marx was convinced, to a failure to recognize the strength of these lines of influence. The 'best' intentions of the 'holiest' will in the world are ineffectual in the absence of suitable social conditions, and these conditions (both the set of existing conditions and, at times when there is a difference, the *possible* set of conditions which would permit of effective action to bring about significant social change) can, at least in principle, be objectively discovered and described: such is Marx's basic approach, so divergent in emphasis from the Christian ethical tradition that culminated in Kant's moral philosophy, to the problem of causation in history and society. Moreover, social outcomes for Marx usually result from a number of interrelated factors, and in particular from clashes of opposing pairs of factors; history, in other words, is not patterned after the simple, sequential causal model of the cue that impels a billiard ball in a single direction so as to strike a second billiard ball, and so on. (The importance of dialectical methodology in determining Marx's adherence to this belief is obvious.) These claims about causality, though in the form in which I have stated them they stand in great need of detailed elaboration, provide useful first guidelines for explaining events from a Marxist viewpoint, and they are in clear contrast with certain other approaches. As generalizations about historical and social causality, they are supportable by vast amounts of evidence. But they hardly amount to a metaphysical theory of causality in general. (For one thing, they do not address themselves to the question of causal sequences in which human beings are uninvolved.) Marx, if I'm not mistaken, has no need of one.

Marxism is a materialism, however; what does this mean, if not that Marx holds certain kinds of entities to exert causal influence, and others not to do so, always and everywhere? What, indeed? Lenin's early philosophical thinking ran along some such lines as these, and so, as a polemical response to the attempt by some self-styled Marxist compatriots of his to fit a phenomenalist epistemology inspired by the thought of the physicist Ernst Mach to Marx's philosophy, Lenin wrote *Materialism and Empirio-Criticism* in support of a general metaphysical theory of materialism of a rather crude kind. It is difficult to deny that, in writing *Materialism and Empirio-Criticism*, Lenin made philosophical claims not to be found anywhere in Marx's work; what disputes there are centre upon whether Lenin distorted Marx (and/or reality) in so doing. Unfortunately for our purposes, many of the standard interpretations of Marx's epistemology for some decades came filtered through the lenses of Lenin's work. I say 'unfortunately', for I am on the side of those who consider that work to have involved distortion.

Marx never leaned very heavily on the 'materialist' label. In his early writings, as I have noted, he preferred to regard himself as a 'naturalist' whose naturalism was at the same time a 'humanism'.

At all times he was anxious, as Engels also was, to distinguish his philosophy from the 'crude, mechanistic materialism' of such eighteenth-century figures as Helvétius and Holbach. In Marx's later writings the term 'materialism' rarely occurs. But Engels bandied it about extensively, particularly in the expressions 'dialectical materialism' and 'historical materialism', and Engels's writings were of enormous influence in the philosophical education of Marxists of Lenin's generation.

The value of the label 'materialism' was in the first instance one of self-identification for Marx; it denoted his resolute opposition to the idealist thesis that thought was ultimately the only reality, with all else being reduced to mere appearance. Its value in the second instance was that of epitomizing and under-scoring the significance, for historical and social explanation, of the generalizations about causality that I have been discussing in outlining Marx's theory of ideology. It precluded him from hypothesizing any alleged transcendental causal agents, for whose existence he found no sound evidence. The 'materialist' label has, in my opinion, little additional use for the philosophy of Marx.

In other words, Marx was not interested in advancing an elaborate theory about the identity of brains and minds, or (after the fashion of the atomists of his youthful studies) about the composition of the ultimate particles in the universe, or anything similar. Were we to admit him to have had such aims, we would have to charge this otherwise meticulous thinker with an extreme carelessness in his manner of pursuing them. It was Lenin who, building upon some statements by Engels, sought to rigidify Marx's principles of historical causal explanation into a set of dogmas to oppose the dogmatic metaphysical theories (the nuanced differences among which he also sought, often in a highly cavalier and unconvincing fashion, to eliminate) of others. In some passages, it is true, Lenin tries to restrict his scope to making modest claims about relative causal priorities, especially in explaining human knowledge processes. In other passages, he stresses the value, as he conceives it, of viewing complex philosophical disputes in a polarized, 'two camps' perspective for the purposes of furthering one protagonist in the class struggle; one may quarrel with his evaluation of this procedure as a tactic, but at least a tactical manoeuvre is less pretentious than a dogma. Finally, however, there are certain passages in which Lenin enunciates dogmas; the following is an example:

Matter is a philosophical category denoting the objective reality which is given to man by his sensations, and which is copied, photographed, and reflected by our sensations, while existing independently of them. (*Materialism and Empirio-Criticism*, Chap. 2, Section 4.)

This sentence, taken along with a few others from the same book, has created a hopeless philosophical muddle for all the (many) latter-day Marxists who have treated Lenin seriously as an interpreter of Marx's philosophy. If, playing down the later clauses in the sentence, one stresses the idea that 'matter' denotes 'objective reality', then few, if any, important thinkers fail to qualify as materialists; idealists, to be sure, tend to make much of the category of 'subjectivity', but that is because, at least to those in the Hegelian tradition, subjectivity (inwardness, the realm of reflective thought— one has a wide choice of synonyms) *is* supremely 'objective', in the sense of being real. If, on the other hand, one interprets Lenin literally to mean that 'matter' refers only to objects directly recorded by the human senses, then surely no one, including Lenin himself, qualifies as a strict materialist, believing only such objects to be real; 'philosophical categories' themselves, after all, are not objects of this sort. Finally, the claim that all knowledge is a more or less perfect or imperfect 'reflection', on the mechanical analogy of a mirror or of a camera, of entities perceived through the human senses eliminates needed subtleties in a wholesale fashion, substituting a highly implausible epistemological and metaphysical doctrine for the web of high-level generalizations about social reality that Marx had woven Lenin's 'reflection theory of cognition', as it has come to be called, makes it difficult to explain (although he briefly attempts to do so) conceptual thinking in general, and in particular the very phenomenon of ideology, the pervasive distortion of reality of a society-wide scale, that Marx had set out to explain and overcome through his observations about the material basis of thought; the same Leninist doctrine replaces the dialectical approach to causality, including the causality involved in perceiving and cognizing, with a simplistic account that is as 'mechanistic' as any from which Marx and Engels had attempted to distance themselves. There are hints in Lenin's *Philosophical Notebooks* that he himself may have entertained second thoughts, late in his life, about his earlier views on matter and knowledge; but *Materialism and Empirio-Criticism* has had a widespread impact on historical interpretations of Marx's philosophy, whereas the *Notebooks* have had little impact up to the present time.

One may, as I do, sympathize with many of Lenin's long-range philosophical objectives in writing his treatise on metaphysics. However, not only was it the case that this area of thought was not Lenin's forte (his unfinished *State and Revolution*, by contrast, contains much that is richly suggestive for political theory), but in addition the whole conception of trying to draw absolutely rigid lines around one's 'materialism', in order to delimit it from the 'idealism' of everyone else, is suspect from a Marxian perspective. Formally speaking, the difficulty with considering Marxism as just one (albeit the correct one, of course) of two or more rival sets of epistemological and metaphysical beliefs is similar to that, discussed earlier, with treating it as just one of several ideologies: Marx claimed to be able to explain the origins of conflicting metaphysical world-wide views, and thus to advance them; and in much of his writing he sought to capture, by anticipation, an atmosphere of social thought in which such conflicts had been dissolved.

In the purest, crudest 'two camps' version (which is cruder, to be sure, than anything to be found in Lenin's writings, but not a great deal cruder than certain passages) of the conflict between materialism and idealism, the protagonists agree, in order to allow the argument to begin, on some common conceptions of two radically different types of entities, 'material' and 'spiritual'. Then, in effect, each side contends that one of these two kinds of alleged entity does not exist. Concessions frequently follow (of course there are such things as ideas, and of course there must be a sense in which bodies are real), until, at the limit, the argument reduces itself to one concerning which of the two types of entities exerts greater causal efficacy. In this latter form the dispute may be productive of information and insight, particularly as additional distinctions beyond the original matter-spirit dichotomy are forthcoming, but in its original version the dispute was sterile and inconclusive. The reason for this was that, in establishing a common ground upon which to struggle, both protagonists had unconsciously conceded too much to the historically dominant tradition of thought about such questions, which is dualism. Both had accepted the conceptual plausibility, while denying the alleged actual fact, of there existing two radically different types of entities. Marx maintains that this very dualistic conception of things, however deep its roots in history, is thoroughly mistaken, though explainable.

The Marxian attitudes towards materialism can best be understood by focusing for a moment on the problem of the one alleged spiritual entity about which the greatest amount of ink and blood has been spilled, God. To the extent to which Marx subscribed to materialism he also subscribed to atheism. (He never took seriously the idea of a material Deity.) In one of his *1844 Manuscripts*, he says the following on the subject of atheism :

[. . .] For socialist man, however, [. . .] the question about an *alien* being beyond man and nature (a question which implies the unreality of nature and man) has become impossible in practice. *Atheism* as a denial of this unreality no longer makes sense because it is a *negation of God* and through this negation asserts the *existence of man*. But socialism as such no longer needs such mediation. It begins with the *sensuous perception, theoretically and practically,* of man and nature as *essential beings.* It is man's *positive selfconsciousness*, no longer attained through the overcoming of religion [. . .]. (*1844 Manuscripts*, 3rd MS., in 'Private Property and Communism'.)

We may set aside the quasi-Hegelian phraseology of the passage and the presence in it of one or two expressions, notably 'essential beings', that Marx would have been unlikely to employ in the same way in later times; what is of importance to us is the thought that Marx is expressing. In a possible socialist society of the future, Marx reasons, it would be unnecessary to take an atheistic *stance,* or position, since the ideology of theism against which atheism is a critical reaction would by then have dissolved and no longer claim adherents. An analogy between what Marx says here about atheism (which accounts, by the way, for the paucity of his comments on the subject) and what he can consistently maintain on the subject of materialism springs readily to mind.

I find the analogy highly plausible. To the extent to which one does, one is able to jettison a great deal of the epicyclical, metaphysical baggage bequeathed us by Lenin and others on the subject of Marxist materialism, and one is left with my original designation of it as a label of self-identification, within the cultural milieu of Marx's time, and as a means of epitomizing or summarizing Marx's highest-level generalizations about historical and social causality, and little else. As Marx's remarks about atheism suggest, the terminology of 'materialism' within the philosophy of Marx should be regarded as provisional, destined to a future dialectical retirement at such time as its successful employment in combat will have eliminated further need for it. For a Marxist who views 'materialism' in this light, there is nothing embarrassing about admitting the meaningfulness of such loose but useful expressions as 'the human spirit', or even about admitting the possibility of certain types of so-called 'psychic phenomena' when evidence for them is forthcoming; for no metaphysical claim about the existence of a world of spirits or souls, radically distinct from the world of material objects in which we ordinarily think of ourselves as living, is entailed thereby. Marxist materialism, in short, as an outgrowth of Marx's theory of ideology and in the spirit of that theory, is primarily a kind of anti-metaphysics, a critique of dominant past metaphysical systems, rather than a new, rival metaphysical system in the grand style.

Prominent in practically all such past systems was some theory about the 'nature of man'. Marx, as a philosopher whose primary concerns lay in the area of human society, rather than non-human reality, had some definite overviews, consistent with the overviews on other general philosophical issues that we have been considering, about the cluster of topics usually treated in such theories. It is to these that we shall now turn, by way of concluding the present chapter.

If there is a single aspect of Marx's philosophy that underwent a significant change of emphasis and even, though to a lesser degree, of conceptual orientation between his earlier and later writings, it is his treatment of 'man'. The change may perhaps best be captured by saying that Marx, if such had been his general custom, would have been tempted to place quotation marks around the word, as I just did, in his later, but not in his earlier, years. The passage that I cited above apropos of the future of atheism will also do very well as an example of Marx's earlier way of talking about 'man'. At the time he adhered to some conception of a trans-temporal human nature or 'essence'—an essence that had become alienated from itself, i.e., rendered incapable of fully realizing its potentialities, in the course of history (which is not necessarily to imply that it had ever actually flourished in unalienated form in some primitive utopia), but that could nevertheless be defined philosophically here and now. Ludwig Feuerbach's designation of man as 'species-being' provided, as I noted in Chapter 2, a linguistic underpinning for this conception. With the *Theses on Feuerbach*, a considerable shift takes place; it is best illustrated by the *Sixth Thesis*:

Feuerbach resolves the religious essence into the *human* essence. But the essence of man is no abstraction inhering in each single individual. In actuality it is the ensemble of social relationships.

Feuerbach, who does not go into the criticism of this actual essence, is hence compelled

1. to abstract from the historical process and to establish religious feeling as something self-contained, and to presuppose an abstract—*isolated*—human individual;

2. to view the essence of man merely as 'species', as the inner, dumb generality which unites the many individuals *naturally*. (Easton and Guddat edition, p. 402.)

This, like the other *Theses*, is a particularly rich text, which can be and has been made the subject of reams of commentary. What is most important for us at this point is its clear implication that Marx will henceforth eschew abstract talk about 'man as such', 'human nature', etc., as much as possible, in favour of making limited generalizations about human beings within specific societies. This is in fact the course that he generally followed in *The German Ideology*, published in the following year, and in his subsequent writings. Rather than discoursing in vague generalities about the historical alienation of man, he became more inclined to specify the conditions and exact kind of alienation that takes place among workers under modern capitalism, for instance, as he does in several passages in *Capital*. The difference between the earlier and later writings in this regard is not one of black and white, to be sure: the *1844 Manuscript* on 'Alienated Labour' contains much that is specific to capitalism and to no other historical system, and the concept of 'alienation' clearly retains considerable importance, as evidenced by a number of texts, in Marx's later thought. But there is a marked shift, nevertheless.

A major casualty of this shift was Marx's adherence, expressed abundantly in the *1844 Manuscripts*, to 'humanism'. As Engels indicates in *Ludwig Feuerbach and the End of Classical German Philosophy*, and as the beginning of the *Sixth Thesis*, cited above, also implies, Marx came to fear that Feuerbachian humanism amounted to nothing but a secular substitute for traditional religion, replacing the worship of God with the worship of Man-as-such. The most obvious practical implication (though not necessarily the implication drawn by Feuerbach himself) of such an attitude was a self-satisfied quiescence totally at odds with Marx's commitment to radical social change. The term 'humanism' connoted so much that Marx found practically undesirable and descriptively misleading that he thought it best to abandon it. This abandonment is to be understood in light of a continuity in Marx's ultimate philosophical aims; he did not suddenly turn misanthrope in 1845.

In fact, the greatest significance of whatever shift there was lies less in Marx's overall view of human beings in their social world than in his way of philosophizing about them. (Or, if one chooses obstinately to identify proper philosophizing with the more traditional notion of it that Marx rejected, then one may speak of a change in Marx's 'way of theorizing'.) Henceforth, he was to be more disciplined and careful in his manner of writing. He was to pay greater attention to language: he had become more aware than before of the ways in which philosophical terms take on lives of their own, so to speak, hypnotizing their users into forgetting the terms' conventional origins and into thinking that they must invariably stand for real entities. (The term 'human nature' is one of the best imaginable cases in point; it has been the careless or hypnotized philosopher's refuge for centuries from the demands of careful social analysis, and it still continues to play that role, among others. The *Sixth Thesis* exhibits Marx's increased recognition of this.) He was to rely much more heavily than before on empirical support for his major claims. Henceforth, in short, in the spirit and style of his writing, Marx was to anticipate many of the best aspects of the stylistic revolution that took place in twentieth-century British philosophy, while avoiding the excessive fear of broad generalizations and of fundamental issues that characterized some of the latter.

Marx's broadest generalizations about humanity across history, to which he subscribed even after having come to perceive the pitfalls of abstract 'essence' talk, are most succinctly captured in a single word that appears in the *First Thesis on Feuerbach*—namely, *praxis*. (It has become customary, among many writers on Marx in languages other than German, to retain the original word as a way of indicating its quasi-technical role within Marxian thought; 'practice' is an adequate English equivalent for it, but 'practice' is so forbiddingly pedestrian and colourless a word as to make the widespread preference for *praxis* understandable enough.) 'Human sensuous activity' is Marx's offhand definition of *praxis*, but this does not take us very far. A more helpful way of approaching what Marx means by it is to consider its role in identifying Marx's overview by way of contrast with others.

In the *First Thesis*, Marx makes this task quite easy. He says, in effect, that there had been something valuable about idealism's conception of human beings: idealism had insisted, against a long-standing tradition that had treated human beings as just one sort of object among all the objects in the universe, that persons are agents, initiators of activity, producers. Of course, idealism had at the same time erred in conceiving of such agency as spiritual, thought-dominated. In discarding idealism Feuerbach has, according to Marx, done well to stress the more fundamental character of the sensuous by contrast with the ideational, but in doing so he has regressed to the ('contemplative') view of human beings as mere objects that Marx attributes to pre-idealist thought. By virtue of this regression, Feuerbach has aligned himself with the ('mechanistic') materialists of the past from whom Marx wishes to separate himself.

Praxis is, then, Marx's way of designating what he called, in referring to Feuerbach's thought, the 'human essence'. But it is highly paradoxical to use this expression in discussing the later philosophy of Marx, for the reason that he has made clear; 'essence'-talk has traditionally conjured up images of some fixed and change-less core, whereas human beings in Marx's world-view are capable, at least in groups, of drastically altering the patterns in accordance with which they act. In the *Theses on Feuerbach*, it will be recalled, 'the essence of man' is said to be nothing grander that 'the ensemble of social relationships' at a particular time.

Nevertheless, the general, trans-societal term *praxis* is not devoid of specific connotations, even if what it connotes is irreducible to a set of fixed qualities. Above all, it connotes human beings' capacity, by contrast with other kinds of entities such as other animals, to effect radical change in 'the world': the relationship between the first of the *Theses on Feuerbach* and the conclusion of the last ('the point is, to change [the world]') is a close one. Moreover, to speak of human beings as primarily 'practical' is to circumvent the language of mind-body dualism, with its traditionally accompanying hierarchical designation of mind as superior to body. Marx makes much of the claim that intellectual and physical activity are not polar opposites; using a properly reformed language, we would no longer be cozened into thinking of them as two fundamentally different kinds of process. Having put dualism behind us once and for all, we would feel no need to downgrade the importance of any kind of productive activity. Whereas classical thought stressed the superiority of intellectual activity, a great deal of such activity in present-day society is considered unproductive according to the rules of the capitalist system. (According to a number of passages that Marx cites from Adam Smith's writings, only profit-yielding activity counts as productive, and very little intellectual activity is profit-yielding.) But neither the classical prejudice nor the capitalist rules need hold in the future. Marx's emphasis on the category of *praxis* thus implies a novel conception, based on empirical generalizations about past history but also applicable to a possible, radically altered future society, of the central importance of *work* and *labour* in understanding human beings.

In addition to one of Marx's footnotes in Volume I of *Capital*, in which Marx straight-forwardly asserts that 'labour is the normal activity of living beings', Engels finds virtue in the existence of two terms, 'work' and 'labour' in the English language. The former, for Engels, is the more generic word, meaning the production of 'use-values', which characterize commodities produced in any era within any economic system; he conceives of 'labour', on the other hand, as being more system-specific to capitalism and as referring to the production of exchange-values. To most speakers of contemporary English, Engels's manner of drawing the distinction is likely to appear rather foreign, but the point that he is trying to make, by way of elucidating what Marx has just said apropos of Adam Smith's idea of labour as being inevitably unpleasant and destructive of freedom and rest, is an important one for understanding Marx's view of human beings: they are *essentially* fabricators, changers—'shapers and fashioners'.

It is useful at this point to recall Hegel's famous depiction of the master-servant relationship, in which this last-mentioned expression occurs, and in particular to recall the significance of the servant's shaping and fashioning activity. It is through this activity that the entire relationship is in fact maintained and the master comes to be seen, in a dialectical reversal effected in the consciousnesses of the two protagonists, as dependent on the servant for the preservation of his very life. The master is an idler who does not labour; we are only carrying out the clear implications of Hegel's own account if we conclude that the servant alone is acting in a way appropriate to the human condition, for only through his activity can human life be sustained. To act humanly, in short, is to work; but the circumstances of work, according to Marx, may be radically different from one form of society to another, so that, *pace* Hegel, even the master-servant relationship itself is in principle eliminable.

In the present, capitalist, form of society, however, as in slave societies and other forms of the past, that possibility is far from being realized. There are masters and servants, known respectively as capitalists and workers. Marx regards the key to the functioning of the entire system as being the fact that the workers' life-activity counts as a commodity, to be bought and sold like any other commodity, within that system. For the major segment of each working-day, the capitalist owns his workers' labour-power—an expression upon which Marx insists in preference to the more ambiguous 'labour'—and has a legal right, within the presuppositions of the system, to use it to advance his own interests. This is the meaning, within the present socio-economic system, of 'alienation': the life-activities of the human actors within the system (even ultimately, of the capitalists, though for somewhat different reasons) are not permitted to remain within their own control, but instead belong to some other person(s) and/or institutions.

Since there is no logical or conceptual necessity that such a system of rights and ownership continue for ever, the much-discussed concept of 'alienation' serves as a clear illustration of my initial contention that Marx's 'metaphysics' is best conceived as a collection of high-level generalizations, justifiable (or not, as the particular case may be) on the basis of empirical evidence, and not as an *a priori*, speculative system of thought. Regarded in this way, the categories of *praxis* and 'labour' are Marx's shorthand terms for higher-level generalizations than that of 'alienation': there is no evidence that human beings need always be alienated, as they are at the present time by virtue of the structural characteristics of their socio-economic system(s), but available evidence militates against conceiving of any future time at which human beings as a group would cease to be workers, shaping and fashioning the world around them, and would become, let us say, the disembodied spirits of religious myth. Despite their being so highly general, however, both *praxis* and 'labour' also have no meaning for Marx apart from their specific historical manifestations, past, present, and projected future. They are only ways of designating certain central characteristics of the human race considered as a prominent, very long-lasting, empirical phenomenon. They do not encapsulate eternal, transcendental truths.

The human race itself may perish. Indeed, as if the machinations of contemporary weapon-makers, military chieftains, and politicians were not enough to convince us, astronomers furnish us with evidence that this is a likely eventuality. Engels, in *The Dialectics of Nature,* shows a profound awareness of the mortality of humanity itself, and finds a kind of consolation in the alleged eternality of nature and its ('dialectical') laws. Such speculation on his part is interesting enough, though fraught with difficulties (having to do with, e.g., the meaning of 'nature', the meaning of 'matter', the relationship between particles and energy, etc.) from the perspective of the philosopher of physical science. This speculation, more than anything to be found in the writings of Marx himself, can be taken to form the basis of a 'Marxist' metaphysics in the old style, albeit a metaphysics of materialism; it has been so taken often enough. But in fact, if I am not mistaken, it is irrelevant to the principal aims of Marx's philosophy, which is concerned with the human social world.

As Marx very succinctly pointed out in the *First Thesis on Feuerbach,* occurrences in the *human* sphere of reality exhibit peculiar characteristics that distinguish them from occurrences in other spheres, even if these characteristics are not best understood under the old rubric of a fixed human 'essence' or 'nature': human beings do not behave in nearly the same way in which either billiard balls or animals do. This observation does not commit Marx to any form of metaphysical dualism, but it casts grave doubt on his occasional, and Engels's frequent, assimilation of the socio-economic 'laws' unearthed by his analyses to the 'laws' of biology and of other natural sciences. Such assimilation, motivated in large measure by a desire to borrow prestige from the enormous esteem in which these disciplines were held at the time, was quite unnecessary in light of the aims and framework of Marx's philosophy. Marx's greatest positive philosophical contribution, as distinguished from his iconoclastic achievements (most notably his theory of ideology), is his systematic employment of certain powerful basic categories, derived from empirical generalizations, for the purpose of illuminating human history and social structures, in particular those of modern Western civilization; by comparison with this contribution, the occasional Marxian hints upon which some of his admirers have seized to erect a new Science of All Reality, called 'dialectical materialism', are of little lasting value. Three of these basic categories, 'alienation', 'praxis', and 'labour' or 'work' have occupied our attention in the concluding part of the present chapter, as we have attempted to clarify Marx's general overview of human beings. We shall proceed to consider a number of other such categories in the next chapter.

5   Descriptive Generalization II: History and Society

It is trivially true that the history of all hitherto existing society has been a history of molecular configurations in motion, or of the stimulations of human beings by pains and pleasures of the most diverse sorts, or of any one of a number of nearly inexhaustible sets of alternative descriptive categories. Marx chose, in the opening sentence of the main text of *The Communist Manifesto,* to focus on class-struggle as a *leitmotif* throughout recorded human history, and in the bulk of his published writings about current affairs and the capitalist economic system he returned repeatedly to the most virulent manifestation of contemporary class-struggle, the opposition between the bourgeois and proletarian classes. But it is important to recall such trivial truisms as I have just mentioned in order to avoid falling into the fallacy that Marx intended his accounts of past and present history and society to be taken as valid to the total exclusion of all other accounts; that would be patently absurd.

If they cannot pretend to exclusivity, what kinds of claims can Marx's accounts of history and society legitimately make upon us? This is no doubt the ultimate philosophical question that needs to be addressed in the present chapter. But before I attempt to deal with this and other issues that require critical examination concerning these Marxian accounts, I am going to summarize a few of their main points. In a book dealing with the historical writings of Marx, or with the economics of Marx, or with the sociology of Marx, various details of these accounts would warrant much more extensive treatment than I am able to provide here. It must be remembered, however, that my comparative inattention to details in these domains is a matter of my own and my readers' convenience, rather than the reflection of any radical division of labour between philosophical and non-philosophical tasks in Marx's thought.

The Communist Manifesto remains, when all is said and done, a very good text to which to turn for enlightenment about the main lines of Marx's description of history. It is condensed and simplified, to be sure, but it is generally not simplistic. Its reputation and its ringing final call for workers to unite have combined to heighten readers' difficulties in seeing it as the complex, nuanced, though somewhat cryptic work that it actually is. In the *Manifesto*, Marx and Engels (it is a joint effort) illustrate their claim concerning history as class-struggle by reference to several pairs of antagonistic groups in earlier periods of history—'patrician and plebeian, lord and serf', and so on. In the modern era, they point out, the greatest power has fallen into the hands of the bourgeois class, the owners of large-scale capital, who are engaged in a struggle to preserve their power against the ever-augmenting class of industrial workers, the proletariat. Both classes have their historical origins, of course, in the events that took place during the feudal period, and their evolution is not yet complete. However, one can discern the outlines of an impending new crisis through an analysis of the nature of capitalist production. The previous crisis was a function of the bourgeoisie's rise to ascendancy: hierarchical and status-based feudal institutional arrangements proved to be obstacles—removable through a centuries-long process of strife—to nascent capitalism's structural requirements that production be continually expanded, markets be established on a global scale, and complete legal equality be made the basis of contractual relationships, which have now come increasingly to be treated as the most important form of human relationships. The historical role of the bourgeoisie, therefore, has been exceedingly revolutionary in its effect on social structures, and it has tended to undermine many of the principal metaphysical illusions that dominated the popular consciousness during the European Middle Ages. Now, through its necessary creation of the peculiar new class known as the proletariat, the bourgeoisie has planted the seeds of its own overthrow.

The modern era has, according to Marx and Engels, several distinctive features by comparison with previous eras of historical crisis—that is, of numerous and intense areas of 'contradiction' or clash within the general social structure. Among such features, in addition to those already mentioned, are the increasingly (but still not exclusively) bipolar character of the modern class-struggle and the built-in, systemic need constantly to intensify workers' productivity by one means or another in order to avert the system's total collapse. This last consideration brings us to matters that are more thoroughly discussed in *Capital* and in Marx's shorter economic writings.

The notion that human labour generates, or creates, exchange-values (as opposed to use-values, upon which I touched in my discussion of Aristotle's influence on Marx) within a society organized on capitalist principles is a keystone of Marx's critical analysis of contemporary society. This general notion was a presupposition inherited from Adam Smith and the others in the tradition of bourgeois political economy, but Marx made use of it to his own distinctive ends. Human labour-power—the *capacity* to make exchangeable products—is bought and sold like any other commodity in the capitalist system; to say this is simply to give an alternative description of the capitalist wage contract. The exchange-value of human labour-power is measurable, at least roughly: it is the quantity of goods and services required to preserve the worker in effective operating condition over a reasonably long period of time, before he or she depreciates. (The need for families, as mechanisms for producing new generations of workers, must also be taken into account, of course.) The minimum such quantity required, which from the labourers' point of view is seen as the subsistence wage, will vary according both to climatic and other natural conditions and to historically modifiable social perceptions of what are to be regarded as minimal 'necessities' of life; hence the inherently approximative character of the measurement. But there exists, as we shall see, a systematic tendency, apt to be offset in individual cases by innumerable other factors (including, notably, the political power of groups of workers organized in trade unions), for all workers' wages to be maintained at a level as close as possible to the minimum exchange-value of the labour-power of the unskilled worker.

In sharp contrast with all other exchangeable commodities, however, human labour-power is, as we have noted, creative: it can, under most circumstances within a capitalist system, readily produce a quantity of exchange-values much greater than its own. In a typical working-day (or week or month—the unit that one selects does not matter), only a certain percentage of the worker's total productive activity is devoted to reproducing his or her means of subsistence—i.e., paying for his or her wages. The remaining percentage is contributed 'gratis', so to speak, to the owner(s) of the means of production that are being used—in other words, to the capitalist(s). But the worker has no genuine choice in the matter, since the only alternative to engaging in this 'surplus labour' and thus creating this 'surplus value', as Marx calls it, is to be unemployed.

The dynamic quality of the total economic system of capitalism is due to the fact that it both facilitates and requires the accumulation of capital (the form of wealth peculiar to this system) on the part of the dominant social class. The predominantly structural, as distinguished from genetic, character of Marx's account in *Capital* becomes evident at this point: *that* the system operates in this fashion, rather than *how* it first came to exist, is the principal issue in which Marx is interested. (The latter, genetic question, Marx indicates now and again, is answerable in terms of such historical developments as the rise of banking in medieval Italy and the uprooting of the English peasantry through the widespread enclosure movement and other related events.) Accumulated surplus value can easily be reinvested by capitalists, in order to provide the basis for even greater accumulation. The resulting need to maximize surplus value entails the minimizing, within the limits of feasibility, of wages. Moreover, multiplying workers' productivity is highly desirable, and this can be achieved in a variety of ways, such as increasing the length of the working day, accelerating the rapidity of their movements, and so on. One of the most obvious such ways is to use increasingly sophisticated technology—mass-production techniques and, ultimately, automation. This contributes further to the tendency towards ever more colossal industries and, at a later stage, towards centralization of large accumulations of capital—in other words, the rise of monopolies and cartels. Owners of capital who are unable (or unwilling) to participate in this tendency are forced to withdraw from the field of combat; thus, like the workers, though for quite different reasons, members of the capitalist class do not have a wide range of choice concerning their methods of operation.

Through the many complexities and nearly limitless variables of the total system, certain fundamental and apparently ineluctable tensions are discernible. One is the paradox that, as automation becomes increasingly prevalent, the basis for the accumulation of capital, which was said to be living human labour-power, must *eo ipso* shrink proportionately; in Marx's technical terms, the 'organic composition of capital', the ratio between the portion of capital investment devoted to raw materials and other similar, non-wage items (factory rental, machinery and so on) on the one hand, and that devoted to purchasing human labour-power on the other, will increase. The effects of this development may be offset for a long time by the enormous intensification of labour productivity made possible by certain types of new machinery, by the fact that technological developments in different industries are highly uneven, by the likelihood that new techniques for extracting raw materials may result in temporary decreases in *their* proportionate costs, and, perhaps most importantly, by the fact that every new, increasingly automated generation of machinery is the outcome of a causal sequence of successive productions of machinery which the labour of earlier generations of human workers set in motion and sustained. Modern capitalism, therefore, is in a sense 'living on its past', while the living-labour basis for its continuation is being eroded. It is not surprising that the possibility of large-scale unemployment is always very real within this system; in fact, according to Marx, the existence and the periodic realization of such a possibility are intrinsic requirements of it. The tendency towards unlimited accumulation of capital renders inevitable the periodic overproduction of goods: not enough consumers with the requisite economic resources exist. Lay-offs and a downward pressure on wages result. The existence of what Marx dramatically calls an 'industrial reserve army of the unemployed', sometimes 'mobilized', sometimes not, thus contributes to the system's functioning. It also generates more intense counter-pressures, in the form of labour union activity and agitation for the establishment of political controls over the capitalist class, from the side of labour.

Many other tensions, either examined by Marx or implicit in his analysis, could be cited. Of major importance in the twentieth century, for instance, are the politico-economic dilemmas resulting from the inevitable expansion of the capitalist system beyond the national and continental boundaries of Western Europe and North America and into the previously non-capitalist regions of the world. The ensuing relative increase in the wages of workers in the advanced capitalist countries, itself a valuable aid to productivity under the sophisticated conditions of contemporary capitalism, temporarily forestalls the possibility of revolutionary activity on the part of this group of workers, but only at a probable high long-range cost for members of the dominant class or their heirs.

But the tension that most intrigued Marx, since it seemed to him most directly relevant to the possibility of there occurring the radical change in the quality of social life that he favoured, was that between the increasingly interdependent, or 'socialized', character of large-scale modern industry and the continued private ownership of the means of production that is required in order for the system to remain capitalist. This glaring tension, he thought, could not be sustained indefinitely; a fundamental change of systems would ultimately take place. It is in projecting this envisaged future event, near the end of Volume I of *Capital,* that Marx wrote one of the book's very few purple passages, now extremely well known: '[. . .] The knell of capitalist private property sounds. The expropriators are expropriated.'

We shall postpone until the next chapter our examination of the elements of predictions of future events that are alleged to be present in Marx's account of capitalism, especially in the passage just cited. At present it will be helpful to consider a sampling of the most common criticisms lodged against the Marxist description of history and society that I have summarized, together with some typical and/or plausible replies to these criticisms, with a view to becoming clearer about the philosophical issues concerning the nature of Marx's account and the sorts of claims to validity that it makes. Serious doubts have been expressed (a) about Marx's emphasis on class struggle in history and especially about the bipolar (some have said 'Manichaean', good-*versus*-evil) character of modern class struggle as he views it; (b) about his reliance on the labour theory of value and his consequent relegation of considerations of *price* to a subordinate position; and (c) about his apparent belief that economic factors have exerted exclusive, or nearly exclusive, dominance over past history, and still do so in present-day society.

(a) A common complaint against Marx is that his insistence on class-struggle is insufficiently grounded in empirical evidence, perhaps even to the point of being 'metaphysical' in the worst sense of that word. In support of this contention, it is pointed out that the opposition between capitalist and proletarian, particularly as it is portrayed in *The Communist Manifesto,* has some of the historically implausible resonances of a high cosmic drama, in which the minor players gradually slip away and the field is cleared for the final, decisive battle between the forces of good and the forces of evil.

Marx does, it is true, make considerable implicit use of the con-

D

cept of 'class', since he frequently identifies 'capitalists' and 'proletarians' as constituting distinct social classes, and these two groups play prominent roles throughout his writings. But his explicit references to 'class' or 'classes' are far less frequent, and what would have been his definitive effort at analysing the structure of the major classes of his time breaks off in mid-sentence after only a few paragraphs; it appears at the close of Volume III of *Capital*. As a result, much of what is alleged by both critics and defenders of Marx concerning his concept of 'class' is mere conjecture. We know, among other things, that he speaks of three prominent classes— capitalists, wage-labourers, and landowners—rather than two in the unfinished fragment in *Capital*; that even in the *Manifesto* he speaks of the existence of other classes or sub-classes, such as the petite bourgeoisie (shopkeepers and the like) and the *Lumpenproletariat* (the 'social scum', drifters who are available to abet the forces of political reaction by serving as paid hoodlums, informants, and so on); and that in his excursions into nineteenth-century French history he often makes much both of the role of the peasantry and of divisions *within* various major classes, such as that between finance capitalists (bankers) and industrialists. On the other hand, it is equally undeniable that Marx and Engels make the following claim near the beginning of the *Manifesto*:

Our epoch, the epoch of the bourgeoisie, possesses, however, this distinctive feature: it has simplified the class antagonisms. Society as a whole is more and more splitting up into two great hostile camps, into two great classes directly facing each other: Bourgeoisie and Proletariat. (*Manifesto of the Communist Party*, Section I.)

The last claim strikes me as intuitively highly plausible when applied to the most advanced industrial societies of Marx's day, but by the same token far less plausible when applied to most advanced contemporary societies. The tendency towards the particular polarization that Marx mentions was very strong then; it has been offset by many factors, which one could name, since. To be sure, it is not yet the case, nor will it perhaps ever be the case as long as recognizably capitalist systems endure, that the 'proletariat' in the sense of 'industrial workers' has lost its place of paradoxical prominence to some other group, as being at once the major active element in producing the goods of advanced societies and yet a comparatively minor depository of their total capital. Nor is it the case, as it appeared to some to be during the 1950s and early 1960s, that the phenomenon of polarization between large groups of individuals is rapidly disappearing from the extant capitalist societies. Nevertheless, I would find it difficult to defend the view that the principal polarizations of the present day, as distinguished from the mid-nineteenth century, coincide precisely and exclusively with the 'simplifying' class polarization of bourgeoisie-proletariat to which Marx and Engels gave pride of place in the *Manifesto*; to do so would indeed, I think, be a descriptive over-simplification.

To imagine oneself attempting to defend such a view is immediately to raise the question as to how one would go about it. For there is, precisely, a considerable ambiguity about the terms, both as used by Marx and as employed subsequently. The term 'proletariat' is probably the best illustration of this ambiguity. As I noted in Chapter 1, part of the force of Marx's later conception of the proletariat stems from his early identification of the mass of propertyless individuals with Hegel's concept, applied by Hegel to an entirely different group, of a 'universal class'. In actual fact, even in Marx's time, 'the propertyless' and 'the industrial workers' were not at all a numerically identical group, and Marx was of course aware of this. Moreover, additional complexities arise when we consider, in addition to the propertyless non-industrial workers (e.g., hired farm-hands) and the small-propertied workers (e.g., certain foremen and skilled craftsmen), such other groups as the small but not negligible band of individuals who are bourgeois by birth and/or propertied but demonstrate by their actions that they are committed to the proletarian 'camp' (e.g., such bourgeois intellectuals as Marx and Engels themselves, who include an oblique self-reference in the *Manifesto*). Surely, under the circumstances, it would be rather futile to begin by procuring the services of a statistician to settle the question, one way or the other.

A portion of our present difficulties in putting claims concerning the polarization of nineteenth- or twentieth-century societies between bourgeois and proletarian classes into decisively verifiable or falsifiable form is unquestionably the fault of Marx's and Engels's excessively dramatic rendering of the situation in the *Manifesto*: dispassionately considered, it contains no explicit Manichaean notion of a battle between good and evil as some critics have charged, and yet it is sufficiently rhetorical to create sizable obstacles to its being dispassionately considered. But we must remember the historical context of the *Manifesto*'s drafting (it was commissioned primarily as a statement of partisan principles, and only secondarily as a scholarly analysis), and we must also consider the possibility, in light especially of the last pages of *Capital*, that Marx would have somewhat altered his rendering of the tendency towards a polarized class division if he had been asked to write a similar piece twenty years later. Another portion of our difficulties stems from one of Marx's greatest historical errors of omission—to wit, his failure to complete any extended, detailed analysis of class structures, and hence of the nature of social classes, before his death. But there is a final set of difficulties, I suggest, that arises from an inherent vagueness, or at least open-endedness, in the concept of social 'class'. One has only to consider the few sample 'in-between' cases that I have just listed; how could a complex modern society ever conceivably evolve in such a way as to eliminate all, or most, such cases?

Ought we then to abandon the use of such concepts in the interests of precision, and radically fault Marx for having failed to do so? I find no compelling reason for drawing this conclusion and several for not drawing it. In making prominent use of the category of social class, Marx is simply meeting his responsibility as a philosopher of history and a social philosopher. That responsibility, as I conceive it, consists in generalizing, with the aid of certain basic interpretative categories that one chooses, about one's subject-matter in such a way as to reflect the actual life-experiences of society's members. Those experiences are, typically, both complex and somewhat confused. The philosophical generalizer must attempt, as best he or she can, to provide a coherent, unified account of them that does not at the same time constitute a denial of their complexity. This is especially important if one's ultimate aim is to explore possible means of radically altering day-to-day social life, as, in Chapter 1, I established Marx's aim to have been.

'Social class' is a very useful category for fulfilling these purposes. It connects the sphere of 'appearances'—the congeries of concepts and ways of thinking characteristic of the everyday world of the ordinary person—with Marx's 'essential' level of explanation, the so-called 'sphere of production'. In systematic interconnection with other categories ('commodity', 'exchange-value', 'necessary labour', 'surplus labour', etc.) employed by Marx in describing the latter sphere, 'class' assumes a preciseness of meaning that it cannot have in day-to-day experience; a certain process of idealization is involved. But there is nothing wrong about this, as long as we can be clear as to what is going on.

On what basis, it may then be asked, might one wish to follow Marx in elevating 'class' to a position of greater importance than any of the numerous conceivable alternatives, such as 'nation' or 'race' or 'sex'? The answer to this cannot consist in anything resembling a deductive demonstration. One may, of course, develop arguments to show that the historical and social role of each of the proposed rival candidates for categorical supremacy in turn is better understood if it is seen as having been influenced, in significant ways, by class divisions. (E.g., the conflicts among modern nation-states are better comprehended if we analyse them in terms of the nations' relative control over present and anticipated future means of production, such as petroleum—a phenomenon that amounts to international class division—as well as in terms of the class divisions *within* the various nations.) Such arguments are often valuable for purposes of clarification, and their likely upshot, as I see it, is to reinforce the wisdom of Marx's judgement concerning the comparative importance of his preferred explanatory category. They are bound to fail, on the other hand, if carried to the extreme of attempting to prove that national, racial, sexual, and other similar divisions have had absolutely no causal efficacy in history that cannot be reduced, without residue, to divisions among social classes. It is of no advantage to Marx's philosophy to make such a claim to *exclusivity* on behalf of the class-struggle account of history and society; the claim of *superiority* in explanation is sufficient. This claim, although it may sometimes be reinforced by detailed arguments, of the sort that I have just outlined, against promising alternative explanatory categories, is best supported by observing the use—consistent, but flexible and nuanced —to which Marx put the concept of class division in his historical writings.

In these writings, Marx imparts intelligibility to such otherwise shocking and seemingly irrational events as the slaughter of the Communards in Paris by the forces loyal to President Thiers. Marx does not try to insist that the Commune was composed entirely of industrial workers and their representatives—far from it. But if, along with him, one understands the actions of the Commune as the effort of a coalition of proletarians, *petits bourgeois,* and some others to alter radically their previous condition within French society *vis-à-vis* the upper classes, which had dominated earlier governments to their own advantage, then one can make sense of the tragic outcome. This is one of many possible illustrations of the usefulness of Marx's concept of class. An extremely good case can be made for its usefulness in understanding even ancient history (a case made long ago by Aristotle, among others, in his analysis of the class basis of revolutions in his *Politics*), as well as for its continued usefulness in understanding the present-day social world. If I am correct in saying this, then no formal proof of the superiority of the concept is needed, even if it were somehow possible to offer one.

At a higher, more abstract level of generalization than that of social class struggle is the idea of human struggle *per se*—of mastery and slavery, of dominance and subordination. Marx often trades on this more generalized approach to the description of history and society (indeed, which social philosopher worthy of the name has failed to do so?), and it is, by definition, 'Manichaean'. (It is impossible to be both master and slave in the same respect at the same time; the one term connotes something positive, the other something negative.) One such occasion is the passage in *The Communist Manifesto* to which I have alluded. But the difficulty with 'dominance and subordination' as a working category for social description is that it applies simultaneously to too many different phenomena of everyday life, thus preserving too much of the confusion characteristic of ordinary social experience. Consequently, 'social class' is preferable, as long as it is not transformed into a magical, supra-empirical entity.

(b) Another fundamental aspect of Marx's descriptive generalizations about history and society that has been subject to frequent criticism is his reliance on a version of the labour theory of value and his consequent stress on the category of value, in particular exchange-value, in preference to that of price. Contemporary bourgeois economists tend, on the whole, to make do without referring to 'value', which was of such central concern to their ideological ancestors of the period prior to Marx's lifetime, and many social scientists and philosophers dismiss as 'non-operational' the notion that commodities have value by virtue of their embodying the labour that produced them.

In order to fully understand Marx's position on this matter, we must recall several elements of his theory that we have previously considered: his overall aim, his methodological reliance on the dialectical interplay of 'essences' and appearances, and his aversion to generalizing about history and society beyond what evidence warrants. It is true that Marx was unoriginal in his view of human labour as generative of exchange-value, but to say this is not to pass any judgement on the validity of the view itself. Marx's basic aim, it must be remembered, was a *critical* one: he found the structures of the everyday life of his society to be radically unsatisfactory, and he was committed to changing them. At the same time, on a theoretical plane, he was radically dissatisfied with the claims to irreplaceability (except by historical regression) made by bourgeois political economists on behalf of the capitalist system that they analysed, and yet he found much of positive worth in the categories that they employed. The critical turn of thought that he took, in accordance with his commitment to fundamental social change, consisted in making use of some of these categories to point up internal tensions and limitations of the system.

Probably no category was of greater importance in this process than was that of 'value'. Adam Smith and his successors had taken as their basic subject-matter 'the wealth of nations' (the title of Smith's book); it was this *wealth* that they sought ultimately to explain by means of their theoretical constructs, and they found in values, masses of them, the key to the phenomenon of wealth. By contrast, it makes neither conceptual nor linguistic sense to regard masses of 'prices' as amounting to social wealth; the widespread buying and selling of goods at agreed-upon prices is, to be sure, the surface manifestation of a condition of wealth and prosperity in a society organized around the principle of commodity exchange, but the prices seem more to be in need of explanation than themselves explanatory. Smith sensed this, thus implicitly relying on a kind of 'essence'-appearance distinction of the sort that Marx, with his keener sense of methodology, made more explicit in his distinction between the sphere of production and the sphere of circulation.

From Marx's point of view, however, Smith was guilty of excessive generalization. In keeping with his assumption, to which I have already referred, of capitalism's historical irreplaceability, Smith had equated the wealth of 'nations' as such with, in effect, capitalist accumulation. In the very first sentence of *Capital*, Marx subtly and carefully distinguishes the object of inquiry of his own book from Smith's much more general putative object of inquiry, and indicates the basis of his criticism of Smith and of the entire bourgeois tradition of political economy; the sentence merits careful reading:

The wealth of those societies in which the capitalist mode of production prevails, presents itself as 'an immense accumulation of commodities,' [Marx cites the opening of his earlier *Critique of Political Economy*] its unit being a single commodity. (*Capital*, Vol. I, Chap. I.)

Marx is pointing out that the capitalist mode of production is based upon commodity exchange, but that not all modes of production need have this basis. His present subject-matter is to be the structures of the historically limited capitalist mode of production, although his aim in presenting this subject-matter is to be, as I have indicated, a critical and not merely a descriptive one. The most general starting-point from which to begin analysing capitalism is the commodity: all goods exchanged within such a system are, by definition, commodities. And, as Marx goes on to argue over the next several pages, all commodities, just by virtue of being exchangeable against definite quantities of other commodities, have exchange-value.

It is because commodities have exchange-values, then, that they can have *prices*. It is because human labour-power is treated as a commodity within the capitalist system and can thus be assigned a certain exchange-value that, after modifications have been introduced to take account of historically fluctuating conceptions of minimum 'subsistence', differences in the skills of individuals, and numerous other factors, labourers can receive *wages*. It is because of the peculiarity of human labour-power whereby, by contrast with all other commodities, it can produce exchange-values greater than its own equivalent value, in the form of surplus value, that *profits* can be generated within the capitalist system.

If, as is the case with many non-Marxist economists today, one's aim is simply to plot the interrelationships between prices, wages, profits, and similar surface phenomena in a system of modified capitalism, then indeed one has no need to refer to 'values'. The complementary concepts of 'supply' and 'demand' then suffice to explain why movement—i.e., exchange transactions—continues to take place at all; one need undertake no deep analysis of the meaning of 'supply and demand', because within the system, the existence of which is not being subjected to criticism, supply-and-demand is a self-explanatory couple. But if, like Marx, one has adopted a critical stance towards the system under examination and wishes to understand it with a view to grasping the real possibilities of its eventual replacement by a radically different system, then a fundamental explanatory category of the type of 'value' takes on great importance. Only a very narrow, inadmissibly dogmatic criterion of empirical verification would deny meaningfulness to this category of 'value', so understood.

It is thus a mistake to claim that Marx's greater reliance on value than on price renders his economics invalid, on the ground that many economists today make do without referring to values. His theoretical aims and his methodology, conforming as it does to those aims, are very different from those of the contemporary economists in question, and hence the categorical generalizations concerning the economic structure of society that he stresses are bound to be different from theirs. This does not imply that he, any more than they, is departing from the empirical evidence to indulge in wild speculation; it is simply that the horizons of his theory are wider.

(By way of compensation for this, Marx's discussion of the mechanisms by which prices come to be established in a market system, while probably sufficient to rebut the charge that he is unable to deal at all with the divergences that are frequently found between actual prices of commodities and whatever values they might conceivably be calculated to have on the basis of his quantitative criterion of the average 'socially necessary labour time' required to produce a given type of item at the existing stage of technological development, is still comparatively programmatic and lacking in detail. When he writes, referring to his own hypothesis: 'The assumption that the commodities of the various spheres of production are sold at their value merely implies, of course, that their value is the centre of gravity around which their prices fluctuate, and their continual rises and drops tend to equalize' [in Vol. III, Chapter X of *Capital*], he is lapsing into metaphor. Metaphor is useful and even, I would argue, necessary at some stage of a systematic explanation of the sort that economic theorists are attempting to devise, but in this instance Marx's metaphor about value as the 'centre of gravity' for prices serves too much the function of a barrier to further elucidation. But then, to repeat, the explanation of how prices come to be set in a capitalist market system is by no means a major objective of Marx's theoretical enterprise.)

Up to this point, I have concluded that it was Marx's theoretical aims that led him to stress value rather than price, and that the legitimacy of his employment of the former category can be upheld on other grounds than the simple historical fact that it was prominent in the writings of the early political economists whom he had read.

'Value' is, precisely, a theoretical category, the product, if I am correct, of a process of descriptive generalization, but not itself the name of a certain class of objects of sense perception. Marx attributes the *creation* of exchange-values, however, to an apparently observable kind of event—namely, the exertion of human labour under certain specified conditions during a certain period of human history. The force of attacks on the allegedly 'non-operational' character of the labour theory of value comes from the obvious impossibility of conclusively demonstrating that, in any given capitalist society of the present day, 'socially necessary labour' and *only* socially necessary labour generates the exchange-values that commodities have. Let us consider further the significance of this for Marx's account of capitalist society.

It has been pointed out, in defence of Marx's reliance on the labour theory of value, that this theory best serves his normative purposes. That is, since the achievement of a classless society is possible only through a radical improvement in the relative position of members of the present working class within the social structure, it is useful to regard them as the victims of exploitation, generating society's wealth and yet not sharing in it, and thus (it may be inferred) deserving of a better lot; the labour theory reinforces this normative point of view. While all of this is true enough, it makes the labour theory sound more like a Marxian ruse, for which writers in the tradition of Adam Smith had unwittingly paved the way, than like the generalized description of the present state of affairs (i.e., of currently existing causal relationships) that Marx intended it to be. Marx, as we shall see in Chapter 7, was reluctant to posit norms, and he was *most* opposed to trying to derive 'is's from oughts'.

Marx's initial argument in favour of the labour theory, to the extent to which he may be said to have one, is an argument by elimination. All commodities have exchange-values, their one and only common measure in the market; what could possibly be the basis for determining the quantitative differences in exchange-values among different commodities? Such superficial candidates as weight, glitter, etc., can be ruled out instantly. A commodity's utility, or use-value, cannot be the basis, either, in the present system, since some of the most useful goods (e.g., air, water) have either no exchange-values or very low ones. (Having some use-value, of course, is a necessary precondition of a thing's possessing an exchange-value, but Marx's point is that its degree of utility, however one might measure this, does not determine its quantity of exchange-value.) In every conceivable instance of a commodity, however, a certain amount of human labour has been exerted in making, procuring, altering, or at least transporting it. And Marx challenges us (desultorily, to be sure, because in his day he had the weight of authority of the bourgeois political economists on his side) to point to an alternative basis for determining exchange-values under capitalism.

What kinds of phenomena might count as alternative bases? Demands, for one. But Marx is successful in pointing out the extent to which potential consumers' demands for goods are conditioned and limited by their place within the existing economic structure of society, as well as the extent to which demands can be created by the expansionary requirements of the system (as exemplified in the historical transition from a dominant morality of abstinence to one of elegance and luxury within the bourgeois class). Demand, then, is a system-dependent phenomenon, and the claim that it is not is ideologically based. *Needs*, on the other hand, do exist in comparative independence of the regnant economic system, although indirectly they are related to it by virtue of the system's role in either promoting or retarding the technological developments that determine the nature and extent of human needs beyond the traditional minimum of 'food, clothing, and shelter' at any given historical period. But the observation, from everyday life, that the capitalist system is distortive of, and frequently fails to meet, human needs, sometimes even to the point of permitting some members of society to starve while others enjoy abundance, is, it will be recalled, one of the starting-points of Marx's entire philosophy; if needs are often not met within the system, then the category of 'need' is clearly unsuitable as a basis for measuring the system's operations. Hence, for someone whose theoretical stance is critical towards the capitalist system, neither 'need' nor 'demand' is useful as an explainer of how exchange-values come into existence within it.

Similar cases can be made against other conceivable candidates for determining the exchange-values of commodities under capitalism, such as the entrepreneurial risk said to have been invested in their production. To the extent to which this means anything more than the exertion of a certain amount of skilled labour, it is the mechanisms of the capitalist system itself that define potentially profitable 'risks' for those who happen to be in possession of accumulated capital. To take 'risks' of this sort, far from manifesting some innate talent for courageous action that might seem to merit a special reward, is simply to act appropriately in accordance with the competitive rules and the internal requirements (in this instance, the requirement to invest or go under) of the system.

Labour, on the other hand, as I noted in the previous chapter, is a continuing fundamental ('natural') human characteristic, which is put to certain specific uses within the capitalist system, without itself undergoing change. As far as the muscular and machine movements are concerned, the production of a given product at the same stage of technological development would be identical within a capitalist economy and any other kind. Thus 'labour' serves as a motive force of the system without itself being system-dependent. If it was meaningful to acknowledge the existence of exchange-values within capitalist economies, then it is equally meaningful to stress the pre-eminent importance of human labour, employed under certain definite conditions, as the generator of these values. Regarded in this way, the labour theory of value is not merely a useful tool with which to reinforce Marx's moral commitment to one side in the class struggle, but also the outcome, like the theory of class struggle itself, of a complex process of descriptive generalization.

Does Marx consider socially necessary labour to be the sole measure of the exchange-values of commodities within a strictly capitalist system? Yes. But in considering the validity of this claim as applied to the actual capitalist economies of the present day or even of Marx's own day, we must not forget the amount of idealization—essential for the elaboration of any rigorous theory, but always potentially misleading—involved in using the term 'capitalist system'. A capitalist system, for Marx, is precisely one that is characterized by, among other things, the dominance of commodity exchange: such basic categories as 'exchange-value', 'surplus labour' and 'capital' are systematically interconnected. Marx's philosophy should be seen as an invitation to apply this systematic and idealized, though empirically derived, network of categories to the existing society, in the belief that it will ultimately explain the experiences of members of that society better than any other conceptual framework.

But just because Marx regards capitalism as an historically transitory form of socio-economic structure, he foresees a time at which the labour theory of value, that bold descriptive generalization about the inner workings of the capitalist form of society, will retain only an historical interest, like his scattered observations about the relations between feudal lords and serfs. In the *Grundrisse*, his posthumously published, middle-period effort at developing the theory that appears full-blown in *Capital*, Marx explicitly envisages an era when heavy industry will have developed to the point at which 'direct labour time' can no longer serve to explain a society's wealth:

As soon as labour in the direct form has ceased to be the great well-spring of wealth, labour time ceases and must cease to be its measure and hence exchange value [must cease to be the measure] of use value. (*Grundrisse*, Notebook VII, Nicolaus (tr.) p. 705.)

From the context, it is clear that Marx regards the possible future society of such an era as being, by definition, post-capitalist. But it seems equally clear, from a consideration of certain basic features about the history of technology to which Marx himself frequently points, that the historical development of what we call 'automated' industry to the point described is bound to be irregular, differing greatly from one industry to another; hence it cannot occur, as it were, in an instantaneous, apocalyptic flash. If this is the case, then any attempt precisely to measure and catalogue all the 'exchange-values', in a given actual society that is in a period of transition to automation, by the standard of 'socially necessary labour' can only be termed quixotic. Indeed, since no society of Marx's own time or since has ever been *strictly* capitalist in form, totally unencumbered by feudal remnants, one is led to doubt whether such a thorough cataloguing of exchange-values could ever have been carried out.

However, since our own society's distance from the limiting-case ideal of fully automated industry remains very great, we should still find the Marxian explanation of the generation of values by the exertion of labour-power, in the present as well as in the now dead past to which we owe our current level of social wealth, a useful tool in explaining salient features of this society that other conceptual frameworks fail to explain. For instance, the remarkable effort to maintain private profits, despite the loss of public amenities and widespread unemployment, during a period of economic crises such as the recent one (1976) in Western capitalist countries makes sense in light of Marx's analysis of the basis of profits in surplus-labour and the systematic necessity that surplus value be maximized, as far as possible, in order to prevent the system's collapse. This is so even though there are certain 'messy' contingent but economically important facts about the present historical situation (e.g., the presence of large petroleum deposits in some geographical regions and of none in others) that Marx never dreamed of mentioning in *Capital*.

If the canons of operationalism in some versions of contemporary social science are taken to require a demonstration of a direct correspondence between a given theoretical category and a denumerable quantity of precisely specifiable items in some actual society in order for the category to be approved as explanatory, then of course the labour theory of value is 'non-operational'. But so is every other comparable generalization, and social theory becomes, in effect, impossible. Marx rejected the idea that his initial justification (in *Capital*) of the labour theory of value was to be taken as a demonstrative proof; the evidence of its explanatory power, he contended, lay in its detailed application throughout his analysis. He does apply it with both quantitative and conceptual rigour. But as an idealized account of the way in which wealth is generated, rather than of the way in which prices are set, under capitalism, the labour theory constitutes a variety of generalization that is very different in kind from the simple amassing of empirical data. This socio-economic theory is, in fact, the best illustration of the complex interrelationship between aim, dialectical method, and descriptive generalization that is characteristic of the philosophy of Marx.

(c) In Chapter 1, I pointed out that Marx's conception of a possible future 'society of associated producers' involved the assumption that, in such a society, the role of what we call economic factors in the lives of individuals would be considerably smaller than it is today. One way of viewing the outcome of Marx's structural analysis of capitalism, aspects of which we have just been considering, is to say that it shows how and why the present state of affairs, so described (i.e., as dominated by commodities, with their relative exchange-values) is as it is. We collectively 'fetishize' commodities, to use Marx's pregnant expression; as individuals living at this point in time, we cannot help doing so. But it need not always be so, according to Marx, in whatever may remain of human history.

A complaint that is frequently made about Marx's accounts of history and society is that his insistence on the dominance of economic causal factors is unwarranted. The complaint itself is clearly unwarranted when extended to Marx's vision of the future; but how well justified is it with respect to his generalizations about the past and the present? In order to answer this question, we must attempt to say just what Marx's contention about the dominance of economic factors amounts to.

Suppose we follow Marx's example, in his famous discussion in *Capital*, Volume I, of 'The Fetishism of Commodities and the Secret Thereof', by considering some of the gross characteristics of feudal society in contrast with capitalism. Marx argues that, although the period of feudalism is labelled the 'Dark Ages', the economic relations and categories of those times were considerably more evident to the members of society than they are in a capitalist structure. Under feudalism, 'services in kind and payments in kind' were dominant forms of economic transaction. Instead of being partially concealed, as they are under capitalism, by the condition of *legal* equality, feudal class-divisions were manifested openly in the serf's working a large part of his time (or, alternatively, a large part of the land that he farmed) for the lord, rather than for himself. Marx concludes:

No matter, then, what we may think of the parts played by the different classes of people themselves in this society, the social relations between individuals in the performance of their labour, appear at all events as their own mutual personal relations, and are not disguised under the shape of social relations between the products of labour. (*Capital*, Vol. I, Chap. I, Section 4.)

In a contrasting capitalist society, in other words, commodities ('the products of labour') tend to exert enormous ultimate influence over members' lives, but they do so in a manner that is not at all obvious to the members in the course of their daily activities.

Just what is Marx implying about the role of economic factors in feudal society? He knows as well as anyone else who has considered the Christian Middle Ages that *religion* exerted a tremendous influence over most facets of Medievals' lives: the great architectural monuments of the period were the cathedrals, built at an enormous cost in human labour; the great philosophical systems of the period, including the standard Medieval economic doctrine of the 'just price', proclaimed their handmaidenly relationship to theology; alleged or genuine disbelievers, if detected and considered unrepentant, were treated as the foremost of criminals and often executed; and so on. Is this an illustration of the *dominance* of economic factors, or of their subordination?

From Marx's critical standpoint, of course, the sets of ideas that were used to justify these salient phenomena of the Middle Ages are ideological myths, unwarranted by available evidence; the social function of Medieval religious objects, institutions, and practices, though far more sophisticated, is comparable to that of fetishes in certain tribal societies, just as commodities are capitalism's fetishes. In order to attempt to understand why daily life in the Middle Ages was as it was, then, we cannot look for any ultimate explanation in the world of spiritual myth itself, and an account in terms of mass self-deception appears hopelessly shallow to anyone who has acquaintance with the period. So Marx invites us to take a look at Medieval property relationships, which were quite different from those that predominate in modern capitalism. While the Defenders of the Faith proclaimed the ultimate reality and ultimate importance of the spiritual realm depicted in their thought systems, they generally justified the existing hierarchical social, political, and legal institutions (including those pertaining to property), or at least maintained that nothing could or should be done to change them, on the basis of this very proclamation. The most dramatic period of transition from feudal to modern society in England was the reign of a Defender of the Faith, Henry VIII, whose contribution to altering property arrangements, through the confiscation of Church lands and other important pieces of legislation, coincided with an important shift in his interpretation of the meaning of 'the faith'. This fact should be highly suggestive to anyone seeking after historical causalities.

But the exact nature of feudal property relationships is not self-explanatory, either. To writers of the Enlightenment, they appeared totally irrational. A retrospective case can be made, however, for their comparative reasonableness in light of such factors as the low level of Medieval technology, the scarcity of known resources, the predominance of rural over urban populations, etc. Needless to say, generalizations about such matters would have to be made with care and greatly qualified with reference to specific geographical regions and to specific periods within this long span of time. The Dark Ages themselves are usually thought of as dating from the barbarian invasions of the Roman Empire; but these events, in their turn, can be explained in terms of the barbarian tribes' own felt needs, rather than being dismissed as entirely non-rational phenomena.

It is along lines such as these, for which the case of feudalism is an interesting and obvious illustration, that Marx intends to lead us in understanding past social history, even though his own detailed historical writing was confined, for the most part, to a few years of the nineteenth century in France. If we consider previous Western history in this spirit of analysing the structures of daily social life at each period and of refusing to accept that period's dominant self-portraits at face value, we shall, Marx believes, be better able to understand how present-day society came to be structured as it is. Historical analysis, however, as we noted in Chapter 3, is not thought by Marx to obviate the need for structural analysis; in fact, he regards the latter as the key to success in the former. Or we could say, alternatively, that Marx takes successful historical analysis to be nothing more than the application of the results of a series of structural analyses to events considered in their actual chronological sequences.

Does all of this amount to an insistence, on Marx's part, on the dominance of economic factors over all others in the explanation of past history? If this is interpreted to mean an ultimate causal dominance rather than a surface dominance, and if 'economic factors' are taken to include such phenomena as the limitations on human productive capacities at given levels of technological development, or the partial satisfaction and partial non-satisfaction of natural human needs in various conditions of relative scarcity, then an affirmative answer to the question becomes plausible. But by the same token the intended referent of the question itself has become little more than a vague slogan, practically useless for philosophical inquiry.

Least of all can Marx be charged with maintaining that economic factors have exerted *exclusive* causal dominance over past and present historical events, unless the connotations of the word 'economic' are broadened so much as to become nearly all-embracing. In Medieval times, as I have pointed out, religious institutions and practices did in fact play an enormous role in ongoing social life, even if we can provide perfectly satisfactory explanations, rooted in non-religious phenomena, for the existence and flourishing of religious phenomena during those times. To label religion, as Marx does in one of his early writings, 'the opiate of the people' is not to dismiss religion's influence as neglible; one has only to reflect on the analogy in light of what we know about the profound influence of widespread drug-use on segments of some contemporary societies. Religious phenomena are just one especially good illustration, political phenomena (institutions, legislation, etc.) being another, of the sorts of causal factors that Marx, in his 'economic' approach to history, is attempting to try to understand, not to spirit away.

I have considered three typical and crucial issues that are often mentioned by way of raising objections to Marx's accounts of past history and present-day society. I have indicated the use to which Marx puts certain basic categories, the products of descriptive generalizations made by him (though often made first by his intellectual predecessors) in the course of his social analysis. I have shown the necessarily limited nature, by contrast with theories pretending either to exclusivity or to absolute certitude, of the claims that Marx is able to make for his network of categories as explanatory of his chosen objects of inquiry; and I have at the same time suggested some reasons for accepting Marx's 'invitation', as I have put it, to understand history up to the present primarily through this network of categories rather than another. Common to much of the criticism that I have considered is the belief that Marx was excessively simplistic and reductionist in his approach to describing past and present social structures; I have demonstrated, I think, that the charge of reductionism must be laid, in far greater measure, at the door of those who hold such a belief.

In short, Marx's philosophy of history and social philosophy, which in the final analysis are inseparable from one another, are highly complex and flexible, rather than, as the facile criticisms would have it, simplistic and dogmatic. Hegel, whose own philosophy of history has often suffered similarly unfair treatment, at least had the 'benefit' of his simplifying hypothesis that history would turn out to be the gradual development of 'spirit' towards greater freedom and reason. Marx inherited the dialectical methodology and certain interpretative categories (e.g., 'struggle', 'dominance and subordination') from Hegel and developed a number of additional such categories on the basis of his own social and historical observations and with a view to his own distinctive critical, philosophical aims. Hegel's hypothesis served to buttress this enormous confidence about the society of his time—it was spirit and freedom fully realized and exhibited in the actual, empirical world—but at a cost: he could say nothing about the future, since he was unable to articulate any further historical tasks for spirit to perform. How, then, was it possible for Marx, lacking Hegel's basis for confidence about either the historical present or the historical future, and dissenting totally from Hegel's positive evaluation of the present, to exhibit the assurance that he did about a favourable outcome in history? How, indeed? It is to this question that we must now address ourselves.

6 Descriptive Generalization III: Prediction

It is my conviction both that the worth of Marx's philosophy is independent of whatever insight it may provide as to what future history will be like, and that an analysis of this philosophy's internal structure reveals no solid ground for enabling one to make assertions, whether true or false, about the future in any but a highly tentative, indefinite fashion. Marx himself, however, would almost surely have taken strong issue with me on this point. Let us examine the reasons.

Two sorts of reasons come to mind: the first biographical and psychological, having to do with Marx's personal history and mental outlook, the second philosophical, having to do with certain underlying Marxian assumptions that can, I think, be successfully separated from the remainder of his thought, to the advantage of the latter. In Chapter 1, I alluded to Marx's habitual optimism concerning the likelihood of an imminent, Europe-wide social upheaval. He expected it, realistically enough, to begin with a political and/or military catastrophe in one or another country— Russia was prominent among the countries that figured in this thinking, as several of Marx's letters attest—and then to spread to others. There were also periods, it should be mentioned, when Marx felt profoundly discouraged about the progress of workers' movements. It would be a mistake to expect to find any overwhelming consistency in Marx's series of guesses about the precise course of historical events in the immediate future. For our immediate purposes, it would also be pointless to draw up a list of these guesses. It is sufficient to note that, by and large, Marx remained confident that a socialist system of one sort or another would eventually replace the capitalism of his day in the major industrial nations, and that this 'eventually' should probably be interpreted to mean 'fairly soon'.

Although developments have been a great deal slower and in some respects less dramatic than Marx expected them to be, there seems little reason to doubt the general correctness of Marx's premonition that the heyday of capitalism, at least in the classic form in which he subjected it to analysis, would soon be past. But there is very little rigour about this statement, and it certainly does not establish Marx as an especially gifted seer. Marx's confidence about the path that future history would take, transmitted to generations of those who have seen themselves as his followers, has certainly had a significant effect in stimulating many of them to engage in revolutionary political activity, since it is gratifying to be 'on the side of the future'; in some, no doubt, it has also had the opposite effect, since a future state of affairs that is absolutely certain to come about may be thought to require no particular individual's assistance in order to be realized. But psychological speculation, whether about Marx or about his followers, must remain of peripheral interest to us here; we are concerned to examine what grounds for predicting the course of future events may be yielded by Marx's philosophy.

In *Capital*, as in most of Marx's writings published during his lifetime, comparatively little is said about the future. Much of what is said about it is couched in the subjunctive mood, outlining what conditions *would* or *might* be like in a 'society of associated producers'; allusions of this sort will be examined in Chapter 7. The remainder, greatly magnified in importance in Engels's less cautious, more sweeping popular expositions of Marx's message, merits close scrutiny. It is epitomized in two well-known sentences at the end of *The Communist Manifesto*, Part I: 'What the bourgeoisie, therefore, produces, above all, is its own grave-diggers. Its fall and the victory of the proletariat are equally inevitable.'

At the close of the somewhat less cryptic, more detailed, but even more rhetorical passage near the end of Volume I of *Capital* that I mentioned in concluding my summary of Marx's structural analysis of capitalism in the preceding chapter, Marx actually inserts a footnote reference to this place in the *Manifesto*. The key sentences in *Capital* read as follows:

The monopoly of capital becomes a fetter upon the mode of production, which has sprung up and flourished along with, and under it. Centralization of the means of production and socialization of labour at last reach a point where they become incompatible with their capitalist integument. This integument is burst asunder. The knell of capitalist private property sounds. The expropriators are expropriated. (*Capital*, Vol. I, Chap. XXXII.)

The two passages together form the core of Marx's serious theoretical predictions (as opposed to casual guesses based on projections from current events), such as they are. The total number of indicative-mood, future-tense sentences in all of *Capital* and the rest of Marx's central theoretical writings is relatively quite small, and none of them have the importance in assessing Marx's claims to being a predictive theorist that his assertions in the passages in question have.

These assertions themselves, it should be noted, are not written in the future tense, but in the non-time-bound present that is a favourite of many theorists. This fact is not very significant in the passage from the *Manifesto*, since to say that an event 'is inevitable' is equivalent to saying that it 'will take place', but I suggest that it may have considerable significance in evaluating the philosophically weightier passage in *Capital*. Let us, then, analyse the two passages in turn, in order to see what conclusions we can draw from them.

On what grounds do Marx and Engels, in the *Manifesto*, assert the inevitability of the 'fall' of the bourgeoisie and the 'rise' of the proletariat? The answer is clear from the context: on the tendency of modern industry itself, against the best (short-term) interests of those who dominate it, to stimulate the development of relationships of association, replacing those of competition, among wage-labourers. The theory, then, is primarily a sociological one, well rooted in the available evidence concerning the beginnings of labour union activity in the industrially advanced countries of the late 1840s, when the *Manifesto* was composed. The technological conditions of modern industry themselves, notably the need to assemble many workers in large factories and industrial centres, were propitious for an increase in such activity, despite generally bitter opposition to it from owners.

As far as it goes, this is not a very exceptional set of claims. But we, with the advantage of hindsight, can raise many questions of interpretation concerning this passage without needing to maintain that any of the assertions made in it are positively false. First and foremost, perhaps, there is the doubt that was to underlie much of Lenin's theoretical and practical activity: suppose the 'revolutionary combination', as the *Manifesto* puts it, of workers succeeds to the point of generating strong trade unions and, correspondingly, a strong 'trade union consciousness' (as distinguished from what Lenin calls genuine 'revolutionary consciousness'), but then stops there? Could there not then be established a sort of equilibrium, unstable, but capable of being maintained indefinitely under certain conditions, between wage-labourers and capitalists? Implicit in this way of posing the first question is a second one: what real difference, if any, is there, from the point of view of members of society with limited life-spans, between an alleged inevitability that is *indefinitely* postponable, and a possible future event that is not inevitable? Finally, what precise meaning is to be attached to the predicted 'rise' (of the proletariat) and 'fall' (of the bourgeoisie)? By what criteria can we be certain, when it is alleged to have taken place, that it in fact has taken place and that, for instance, the exploitation of wage-labourers by capitalists has not simply given way to a new form of class-division under which the modern Western legal institution of private property has been abolished but other important features of the former relationship between bourgeoisie and proletariat have been retained?

The longer passage in *Capital* serves, not to resolve these questions to anyone's total satisfaction, but at least to indicate more of the basis, in descriptive generalizations about trends occurring in the most advanced society of his day, of Marx's projection concerning fundamental social change in the future. This passage is correctly seen, I think, as the terminal point of Volume I, the only volume completed in publishable form by Marx himself, even though there is one brief subsequent chapter. (The latter concerns colonization, and was no doubt inserted partly with a view to considering one possible road to survival for capitalism—a road exemplified primarily by the United States, with its atypical but by then rapidly diminishing conditions of abundant virgin soil and an under-supply of labour—and partly with a view to lulling hasty censors, by its comparative blandness, into letting the book pass.)

Prior to the passage in question, Marx has quickly summarized a few of the main historical developments which contributed to the genesis of modern capitalism—the process that the bourgeois political economists had denominated 'primitive accumulation'. He now proceeds to draw both contrasts and parallels between the latter process and the one that he foresees—or rather, to express it more accurately in light of what he says elsewhere, that he sees as already having begun. Both processes involve expropriation. In the earlier one, which has presumably still not been brought to full completion everywhere in the world (certainly not in Marx's time, at any rate), those engaged in small-scale industry and agriculture were compelled, by the forces of the burgeoning market economy, to yield control over the means of production to successful large-scale capitalists. Often, as in the classical early instance of the destruction of the English yeomanry, considerable violence, frequently supported by legislation of the most repressive sort, has characterized this expropriation.

The denouement to Marx's visionary utterances about the expropriation of capitalist expropriators is interestingly anticlimactic. He concludes the chapter in which these utterances occur by saying that the earlier process, that of capitalism's development, 'is, naturally, a process, incomparably more protracted, violent, and difficult, than' the one that is, presumably to come. (I say 'presumably' because it must be remembered that Marx writes of the projected future historical process in the atemporal present tense.) He explains this reasoning in terms of numbers: in the first case, many were expropriated by a few, whereas the reverse would be true of a transition to socialism. This sheds a great deal of light, I think, on Marx's confidence concerning the future, particularly if one brackets the final chapter on colonization and conceives of the two-sentence paragraph in which these remarks are made as being, in effect, Marx's last word in his *magnum opus* of 1867. Comparatively quick, pacific, and easy: such is Marx's expectation concerning the transition that he both foresees and hopes for.

It seems superfluous to say it: there is precious little basis for confidence in Marx's reasoning on this issue. What is worth stressing, however, is that such scepticism finds abundant justification within Marx's own critical conceptual framework, even if Marx and most contemporaries sympathetic to him were too much impressed by what they considered the favourable signs of their times to realize this. Marx succeeded, in his analysis of capitalism, in developing a number of descriptive generalizations on the basis of certain categories that he selected. He provided solid, impressive data to support his claims that the numbers of units to be included within certain major categories were increasing relative to others—for instance, that, in general, the ratio of variable capital (wages) to constant capital (raw materials and other investments) in advanced industries was changing in the latter's favour. But he also, quite rightly, identified a sufficient variety of quantitatively variable categories to prevent, logically speaking, the drawing of any *certain* conclusions about the total dominance of any one or two trends over all the rest within an indefinitely extended future time-period.

Let us take, for instance, the trend towards 'centralization of the means of production'. It, together with 'socialization of labour'—i.e., the fact that modern industry is coming increasingly to depend on complex, co-operative networks, often global in scale, for its continued functioning—is a phenomenon that Marx identifies as leading to capitalism's downfall, in the sense that its incongruity with the capitalist institution of private ownership will become increasingly apparent to increasing numbers of workers, the ever greater mass of the population. But Marx himself points out elsewhere (*Capital*, Volume I, Chapter XXV) that the centralization of capital is not the same thing as its accumulation or concentration, for accumulation is often accompanied by an actual increase (through inheritance and other, more complicated processes) in the numbers of individuals who are capitalists. He does maintain that 'centralization completes the work of accumulation'—a vague claim, though one that appears very plausible in light of the growth of gigantic national and international enterprises in capitalist countries during the present century—but he goes on to say that this completion can be accomplished either through the more violent method of one company killing off its competition or through the smoother method of forming joint-stock companies. He offers no proof, nor can he, that centralization must inevitably be so thoroughgoing as to reduce the actual or even the relative numbers of capitalists to the point at which expropriation of their holdings by the working class would be the easy matter that his concluding remarks imply it to be. Moreover, his references to the advantages (those of 'smoothness') of forming joint-stock companies suggest a method whereby, temporarily at least, centralization and augmenting the numbers of capitalists can be promoted simultaneously.

To say this much by way of mitigating, through a use of Marx's own generalizations about capitalism's basic trends, his assurance concerning the 'inevitability' of a quick and easy transition to socialism is of course to neglect many other trends that he analyses as taking place along with that of centralization; some of these trends, it might be said, serve to reinforce this assurance (whether or not we consider Marx's descriptions of them to have been accurate). But that is just the point: some reinforce the ultimate conclusion concerning an inevitable transition, some mitigate it, and the entire, interdependent system, as delineated through Marx's conceptual framework, is much too complex to permit its future development to be summarized, in advance, in a stark prediction of the inevitability of its demise in the manner asserted (expropriation of capitalist holdings by the mass of workers).

A full analysis of the ins and outs of the few sentences, leading to the 'prediction' of expropriation of the expropriators, upon which I have been focusing, would lead us into many fascinating by-ways. One, of great historical importance for understanding a certain disenchantment with Marx among European socialists that began with the writings of Eduard Bernstein near the turn of the century, has to do with the claim, made in the context of both the *Capital* and *Manifesto* passages that I have singled out, that a trend towards at least a relative, if not an absolute, 'impoverishment' or 'immiseration' (with respect to living conditions) of the members of the working class is discernible. This claim, which is nowhere discussed explicitly in very much detail by Marx (though it is implicit in his choice of numerous reports about shocking conditions in factories and mines in his time that he reproduces in *Capital*), raises in its turn many more questions. (E.g., what are the criteria of impoverishment? To what extent can it be mitigated or even reversed in advanced countries by imperialist policies abroad? How can we be assured that the masses' perception of their increasing relative impoverishment will inevitably lead to their taking decisive action against the owners of the means of production? etc.) At least on a superficial level, and with reference to workers in the advanced industrial countries, it seems clear that the thesis of 'immiseration', if Marx intended it as a prediction about the near future, is implausible. In any event, we are here most concerned with the philosophical issue of the significance of the alleged predictive aspect of Marx's philosophy, and we must forgo further pursuit of such by-ways as this.

Before proceeding to draw additional conclusions, I must mention one further trend about which Marx wrote in considerable detail, a trend that is frequently singled out as having the greatest influence on his anticipation of the capitalist system's immanent breakdown. It is, as the curious and revealing title of *Capital*, Volume III, Part III calls it, 'The Law of the Tendency of the Rate of Profit to Fall'. That there was a significant decline in the profit rates of many major industries, from their first flushes of success in the early stages of the Industrial Revolution to the period of Marx's maturity, was hardly a discovery on his part. It had greatly concerned Adam Smith's successors, and, as Engels makes plain in the Preface to his first edition of this final volume of Marx's major work, it was a trend that some critics had declared Marx incapable of dealing with, on the basis of his Volume I. Marx's mathematical explanation of it is elegantly simple. Let s represent 'surplus value', v 'variable capital', and c 'constant capital'. The 'rate of surplus value' or, to use an equivalent but more emotionally charged phrase, 'rate of exploitation', is defined as s/v; the rate of profit is defined as $s/(c+v)$. If, as Marx has already (in Volume I) shown to be the general case with the advance of technology, the ratio of v relative to c within total capital investment declines, and if s/v remains constant, then $s/(c+v)$ must necessarily be reduced in magnitude.

But of course, before one can translate this obvious mathematical conclusion into a prediction of an irreversible actual trend with a definite (and not simply asymptotic) terminal point in the future, one must be able to validate a great many assumptions. To do this with complete assurance turns out to be impossible. The two most evident assumptions, in the present case, are those concerning (a) the constancy (more or less) of the rate of surplus value and (b) the ratio between constant and variable capital. If, for instance, the rate of surplus value should be greatly multiplied by an enormous jump in workers' productivity, accompanied by little or no increase in the value of their labour-power (v, their wages), then clearly the trend towards a diminution of $s/(c+v)$ would undergo a reversal, at least in the short term. Marx himself alludes to this possibility, though in an unwontedly hasty fashion, in a sub-section entitled 'Increasing Intensity of Exploitation'. It is one of six possibilities that he enumerates, that of 'Cheapening of Elements of Constant Capital' (i.e., an alteration in the basis of assumption (b)) being another, under the general heading 'Counteracting Influences' (to the Law of the Tendency of the Rate of Profit to Fall). The other four influences, which I list for completeness' sake, are: depression of wages below the value of labour-power; relative over-population; foreign trade; and the increase of stock capital.

In the single paragraph in which he introduces this discussion of countervailing factors, Marx asserts that, given the tremendous growth of modern industry since about 1850, the fact that the rate of profit has not declined more swiftly than it has stands equally in need of explanation with the decline itself. It is for this reason, he adds, that he has called the phenomenon a 'tendency', since it must be these countervailing factors that have given '[the general law] the characteristic of a tendency'. This is an enormously important admission on Marx's part. Tendencies can be contravened. And yet, oddly enough, he does not simply drop the terminology of 'general laws', either in the title of the section or in the explanatory text.

It is in this terminology and in the way of thinking about the world that lies behind it that we must locate the theoretical basis upon which Marx was able to buttress his attitudinal optimism concerning the prospects for an imminent transition to socialism. In the Preface to the first edition of *Capital*, Volume I, Marx declares it to be 'the ultimate aim of this work, to lay bare the economic law of motion of modern society', and he clearly identifies this 'law' or set of 'laws' with 'natural laws of . . . movement'. It is unreasonable to doubt that Engels, attuned as he was to natural sciences and to those sciences' own self-images of the time, played a role in influencing Marx to use this terminology more frequently; it is equally unreasonable to absolve Marx of all responsibility for it.

To have used it was in any event a mistake. For the language of 'natural laws', the operation of which is said to be irresistible, fosters a conception of a simply and rigidly determined social world that is at odds with the logical conclusions of Marx's analysis. True, Marx himself immediately acknowledges, after referring to these alleged laws, that an awareness of them 'can shorten and lessen the birth-pangs' of a society's natural development, presumably in the direction of a post-capitalist social structure. But he still speaks of the laws or, even worse, *the law* of modern society as if it were a real abstract entity, hitherto hidden behind the phenomena of capitalism, and now for the first time brought to light in his work. Conceptually and historically linked with, though perhaps not strictly entailed by, this idea of rigid, 'pitiless' social laws is the metaphysical thesis of strict determinism. And if someone believes both that he or she has a clear grasp of the law of movement of society and that strict determinism prevails in the universe, then that individual is prepared to set up shop as a forecaster of the course of future events.

What I showed in Chapter 4 concerning the superfluousness, for his basic aims, of Marx's erecting 'materialism' into a metaphysical dogma of the sort to which Lenin and other followers have subscribed applies equally to a metaphysical dogma of determinism. It may or may not be the case that, given a detailed knowledge of the position of every particle in the universe at time *t*, we could accurately predict all positions at time *t+n*; the question is in principle undecidable, and in any case it is irrelevant to Marx's purposes. Marx wasted no time in attempting to elaborate such a dogma in detail (although Engels's *Dialectics of Nature* includes some fairly indecisive and unproductive pages about the resolution of freedom and determinism), and he shows great impatience with the inflexibility and rigid, suprahistorical determinism implicit in the phrase 'iron law of wages', upon which the dominant Lassallean faction placed such stress in drawing up the Gotha Programme of the German Social Democratic Party. Marx would have done well to be similarly critical of his own conception of 'the economic law of motion of modern society', even though it is supposedly restricted to a single historical period.

Beyond the generalization that regularities, including certain specifiable sorts of causal regularities, obtain in the interrelated regions of phenomena (economic, social, political, etc.) that concern him, Marx requires no theory about the strict predictability of future social events to underpin his analysis. (If one chooses to call such a broad generalization as the above a theory of 'determinism', then so be it; it is then simply a matter of terminology.) If this analysis is successful in providing a coherent, systematic explanation of the phenomena in question, together with descriptive generalizations of salient trends within them and a basis for understanding why certain of these trends may already (since Marx's day) have been reversed over either a short or an indefinitely long term, then that is enough to make it valuable in light of Marx's own aims. (It is also enough to enable us to call the analysis a 'scientific' one, in the broad sense in which this word is usually meant in its German equivalent, '*wissenschaftlich*', and in our English expression, 'social science'.) Nothing more is needed to provide us with a theory that is at once explanatory and, given the nature of Marx's findings, critical.

In stressing the separability of strict predictions about the future, to the (at most, very limited) extent to which there can be said to be any such within Marx's writings, from the rest of his thought, I have necessarily dwelt in this chapter on certain difficulties inherent in Marx's claims about existing trends, as well as on the more general philosophical problems surrounding the question of social and historical prediction. This emphasis of mine should not blind the reader to the remarkable degree to which Marx did in fact identify and describe trends in the constantly modifying system of capitalism that still, and in some cases increasingly, characterize it in its present form—e.g., its periodic crises of overproduction, its reliance on an 'army' of now potentially, now actually, unemployed workers, its development in the direction of monopoly capital, and so on, not to mention the broader areas in which capitalism's strictly economic mechanisms determine the nature of non-economic relationships and institutions in modern society. But it is precisely because Marx had a keen sense of the complexities of the subject-matter with which he was dealing in *Capital* and his other economic writings, including especially an awareness that political legislation and other social changes advocated by the system's victims as a means of mitigating its harshest effects might conceivably result in a significant modification of the original system itself, that his philosophy is misunderstood if it is presented as strict prophecy.

7   Vision of a Possible Future

We come now to the final aspect of Marx's philosophy in accordance with my tripartite division of methodology, description, and norm. This final aspect is also the most paradox-laden. The most salient paradox is to be found in the juxtaposition of two facts: first, that Marxism is clearly more heavily oriented towards a social ideal (or ideals) than almost any other important system of philosophical thought in the past century and a half, and second, that Marx disdained ideal-mongering and wrote relatively little about the features that he would expect to characterize future society. Further paradoxes arise in attempting to explain this one.

Engels, in an essay that has become justly acclaimed as a succinct though often dubious introduction to Marx's thought, lays down the gauntlet to those who (whether with benevolent or malevolent intent) claim to discern a host of social 'oughts' in Marxism. The essay's title is *Socialism: Utopian and Scientific*, and in it Engels attempts definitively to separate the scientific Marxist sheep from the utopian goats; indeed, Engels had a good deal to do, as an intellectual historian, with affixing the label 'utopian socialist' to the three objects of his special attention—namely, the Comte de Saint-Simon, Charles Fourier, and Robert Owen. The immediately apparent ground on which Engels draws his very sharp (untenably so, as I think it is easy to demonstrate) distinction is Marx's success in discovering the 'secret' of capitalist production through his theory of surplus value and in combining this with a materialist theory of history. But a closer analysis of the structure of Engels's argument reveals that there is another, and I think somewhat more persuasive, reason for maintaining that Marx cannot be regarded as just one more individual in the tradition of early nineteenth-century socialist thinkers, with perhaps a few turns of thought peculiar to himself: it is that he, unlike his predecessors (except for Owen in the final stage of his career), recognized that a transition to socialism could not be achieved without acceptance of the fact of class-struggle and widespread activity on the side of the presently subordinate class. What characterized the utopians, by contrast, was an attitude of hopeful expectation that social structures could be changed radically by means of an accretion of mutual good-will and understanding.

There is an irony involved in this way of viewing Engels's dichotomy between scientific and utopian socialism. For, in the nineteenth century even more than in the twentieth, the conception of the scientist as a dispassionate, uninvolved, 'objective', observer of his subject-matter was extremely prevalent; its influence on Marx, particularly in some of the 'predictive' passages discussed in the preceding chapter, was considerable. Yet we find Engels, who was much more strongly affected than Marx by his century's dominant attitudes concerning science, ascribing the deficiencies of the 'Utopians' precisely to their fantastic 'standing apart from the contest'. (This phrase actually occurs in *The Communist Manifesto*.) He conceives of truly 'scientific' socialism (i.e. Marxism), on the other hand, as being involved and committed, rather than detached.

Commitment to one side in a struggle must, if it is to be intelligent, be accompanied by some sort of conception of a goal that one wishes to be the outcome of the struggle; the only alternative is blind combat for combat's sake, a stance that, at its limit, becomes incommunicable and unintelligible. The goal in question need not be regarded as fixed or final. Marx's goal, as I shall argue, is neither. But the philosophy of Marx assuredly does include a social goal or 'vision', as I have called it, without which any presentation of his 'scientific socialism' will be truncated. This element is neither logically disconnected from nor deductively related to the descriptive aspects of Marx's thought; the situation is more complex than either of these extreme alternatives. And since I have cast so much doubt on the idea that Marx could claim, even on his own premises, the ability to predict with confidence the course of future history, I think it appropriate to speak of Marx's normative vision as one of a *possible*, as distinguished from a certain, future.

The number of passages in Marx's writings in which this vision appears is small but, I think, decisive. There are, first of all, a number of pages in the *1844 Manuscripts* in which Marx waxes eloquent to the point of obfuscation concerning the overcoming of alienation and of the institution of private property and concerning the new types of functions that would become possible even for the human senses in a communist society. There is, secondly, the frequently cited, tongue-in-cheek passage in *The German Ideology* in which communist society is described as one in which one could 'hunt in the morning, fish in the afternoon, breed cattle in the evening, criticize after dinner, just as I like, without ever becoming a hunter, a fisherman, a herdsman, or a critic'. Then there is the *Critique of the Gotha Programme,* in which Marx subscribes to the old socialist formula, 'from each according to his abilities, to each according to his needs!', as an appropriate distributive principle for the form of socialist society that is possible in some distant future, though by no means immediately attainable. (For the time being, Marx believes, compensation will have to be paid according to one's work.) None of these passages, it is interesting to note, was edited by Marx with a view to their circulation among the general public; even the *Critique of the Gotha Programme* was written as a private letter. Lastly, however, there are occasional references in *Capital* to a possible future 'society of associated producers', and these can at least be said not to contrast jarringly, in their substance, with all the then unpublished but now better-known material.

The passages in *Capital* are, on the whole, rather undramatic and very general. Many are couched in the future subjunctive mood or introduced with such hypothetical language as 'Let us picture . . .'. The words 'social', 'free', and 'rational' appear frequently in them. Marx speaks of his possible future society as involving more rational planning in both the production and the distribution of goods, fuller utilization of scientific and technological advances (because the issues of their immediate profitability would no longer be uppermost), the opportunity for more well-rounded development of the talents of individuals, and the amelioration of relations between the sexes and among the generations. Probably the best-known of these passages occurs near the very end of *Capital,* Volume III; it is at once lyrical and sober-minded:

Freedom in this field [that of the satisfying of wants, which them-selves increase with the development of civilization] can only consist in socialized man, the associated producers, rationally regulating their interchange with Nature, bringing it under their common control, instead of being ruled by it as by the blind forces of Nature; and achieving this with the least expenditure of energy and under conditions most favourable to, and worthy of, their human nature. But it nonetheless remains a realm of necessity. Beyond it begins that development of

E

human energy which is an end in itself, the true realm of freedom, which, however, can blossom forth only with this realm of necessity as its basis. The shortening of the working-day is its basic prerequisite. (Chap. XLVIII, Section III.)

If we assume, as seems reasonable, that the sentiments expressed here are Marx's and not just those of Engels (who claimed to have found the section in which this passage occurs complete, though in first-draft form, after Marx's death), then this notion of a 'realm of freedom' can be said to have been the touchstone of Marx's vision of a possible future from the start (in the early manuscripts) to the finish of his philosophical career.

By way of embarking upon a consideration of this vision, I wish to confront the issue as to why Marx was usually so fearful of discussing his aspirations for the future of humanity. Several seemingly promising explanations of this phenomenon prove to be unsatisfactory. David Hume's point about the logical impossibility of deducing prescriptions from descriptive statements may have had some indirect influence on Marx, but on the whole Marx paid little attention to formulations concerning basic problems about morality that have been prominent in the British philosophical tradition. On the other hand, Hegel's systematic refusal to pass ultimate value-judgements on the various 'moments' described in his *Philosophy of History*, except from the standpoint of each stage's relative contribution to the final goal of complete and rationally exercised freedom, undoubtedly imparted a peculiar sort of intellectual discipline to Marx's thought that remained with him throughout his career. But Hegel refrained, except for three or four isolated passages inserted in unguarded moments into that posthumously edited work, from indulging in any speculation whatsoever about the future, even about a *possible* future, whereas the same cannot be said of Marx. Finally, Marx, like Engels, conceived of himself as 'scientific', and no doubt the then inchoate ideal of 'value-free social science', later to be elaborated in detail by that close student of Hegel and Marx, Max Weber, was already becoming fashionable in Marx's time. But this last explanation for Marx's attitude about social goals is also inadequate, since Marx as a thinker was usually not prone simply to follow the prevailing fashions.

The basic reasons for the dearth of references to the possible socialist society of the future in Marx's published writings are, it seems to me, two: first, Marx was profoundly contemptuous of the ideological use to which moralizers of various political shades routinely put key value terms; second, he was profoundly aware of the unreasonableness of conceiving of socialist society as a fixed, immutable 'state of affairs', the structure of which he could with confidence delineate in advance. I shall discuss these points in order.

Such common evaluative terms as 'goodness', 'justice', and 'rightness' are conspicuously rare throughout Marx's writings. Marx seemed to feel, as I noted in Chapter 4, that the only non-ideological use of such terms was to designate what took place in accordance with the rules, themselves always exploitive in the sense of supporting the dominance of one or more groups over others, of a specific past or present socio-economic system. Beyond that, he believed, the terms had traditionally been used to encourage the most widespread possible acceptance of the rules at any given period. Those numerous so-called 'socialists' who attempted to argue for the superiority of their aspirations by labelling their projected future societies as 'better' or 'more just' than those of the past were, in effect, playing the same intellectual game as the ideologists whom they opposed, in Marx's view. Such 'arguments', however well concealed under serious and high-sounding phrases, were no arguments at all, but merely sermons.

It should be remembered that 'morality'—meaning, as I take it, moral philosophy of both the academic and the 'conventional wisdom' sorts—was one of the types of theoretical enterprise that Marx and Engels explicitly listed as examples of 'ideology' in *The German Ideology*. The implication of this for the stance taken towards ethics or moral philosophy by the philosophy of Marx is as clear as it is uncompromisingly radical in principle: what is proposed is the elimination of moral philosophy, not the substitution of a new moral philosophy for the old ones. *There is no Marxian ethics, in the traditional sense of cataloguing hierarchies of values and proscriptive rules of conduct of assertedly universal validity.* This does not, of course, preclude the existence of a Marxian theory *about* ethics as an intellectual enterprise; the theory of ideology is just such a theory.

It is no violation of Marx's fundamental stance towards ethics if he points, as he does on occasion, to ineluctable inconsistencies either between the theory of justice espoused by ideological defenders of, let us say, capitalism and actual capitalist practices commonly held to be just, or else among various elements of a given theory of justice. In such instances, Marx is simply employing the common technique of internal criticism—often to devastating effect. The same technique is being used when Marx elaborates on the contrast, so pivotal to the entire argument of *Capital*, between the legal, contractual (but, as Marx wishes to insist, relatively 'abstract') freedom of the worker and his actual unfreedom, in the sense of his comparative powerlessness and dearth of genuine, concrete alternatives, in the typical employment relationship within capitalism. But there is, as I noted parenthetically in Chapter 4, an important difference between Marx's treatment of 'justice' and his treatment of 'freedom'. This difference is also a potentially disturbing one. For there are contexts, such as the passage that I have cited concerning the minimization of the realm of necessity in a possible future socialist society, in which Marx, like Engels, uses the term 'freedom' in a very positive sense, to designate one of the crowning features of his social vision. By contrast, he never refers to the society of associated producers as 'the realm of justice' or even as 'a [pre-eminently] just society'.

Does this imply that Marx has simply failed to 'pull off' his radical rejection of the enterprise of moral philosophy, and that he has substituted a predominantly freedom-based ethic for a predominantly goodness- or justice-based ethic? There is just enough truth to this manner of stating the case as to render it incapable of dismissal out-of-hand; to recognize this is to understand the genesis of the numerous glib references to a 'Marxist ethic' in the writings of Marx's defenders and opponents alike. But such references amount to a trivialization and a serious misrepresentation of the entire normative aspect of the philosophy of Marx.

In opposition to the attempt to reduce Marx to the status of just another moral philosopher in spite of himself, a case can be made for there being an important difference in kind between the primarily critical enterprise in which Marx is engaged, in which the word 'free' is occasionally used as an open-ended way of characterizing a society from which the restrictive present-day phenomena that are the objects of his criticism would have been eliminated, and the more value-postulating enterprise involved in developing an ethical theory of a 'just' (or of a 'good') society. The former is essentially, at least in intent if not always in actuality, descriptive in its approach to normative matters. In other words, Marx generalizes about existing restraints on certain human activities, and he then occasionally refers, by contrast, to one or more possible societies in which these restraints would no longer exist. The latter enterprise, that of constructing a model of a just society (whether an ideological model intended to identify elements of past or present social practices with the ideal of perfect justice, or a 'utopian' socialist model), is necessarily far more stipulative than Marx's, since outside of predefined notions of what is just and unjust there is no empirically specifiable synonym for 'injustice' that is comparable to 'restraint', used as a synonym for 'unfreedom'.

But it would be fatuous to attempt to absolutize this distinction between the way in which Marx sometimes relies on a notion of freedom and the way in which more traditional moral philosophers depend on notions of goodness and justice. Marx himself was certainly not always as careful as he might have been, even in his later writings, about avoiding the stipulative or 'moralizing' use of value-laden terms, including 'freedom'. What is more significant, however, is his general consistency in the matter, rather than his occasional lapses. On the whole, it is safe to say, Marx manages to have something to say about many of the central problems with which moral philosophers have traditionally grappled, while only very seldom resorting to the language that they have traditionally employed. I have given, as the first reason for his taking this approach, his and Engels's profound contempt for the ideological posturing (and even, one should add, the intellectual dishonesty) that is intrinsic, as they saw it, to stipulative moralizing. The other principal reason has to do with the nature of his vision of a possible future society that he personally regarded as probable or even certain to come about; the comparative dearth of traditional ethical language in Marx's later writings enhances the value of these writings as, at least to a slight degree, revelatory of the manner in which Marx conceives of the envisioned future society itself—a society in which moral philosophy would no longer serve any function, because the restrictive features of present-day society would have been abolished. Let us now turn our attention to this central issue.

In the passage from *Capital*, Volume III, that I cited earlier in this chapter, Marx makes a rare use of the expression 'human nature', when he speaks of the condition of human beings in the 'realm of freedom' as being one 'most favourable to, and worthy of, their human nature'. There is a sense, then, in which the hoary concept of 'human nature' retains its traditional status as a normative ideal in the philosophy of Marx. (This is true even though, as I suspect, Marx might have been inclined to eliminate this expression as potentially misleading if he had had the opportunity to complete the editing of his work.) But it is equally true that Marx never renounced the insight, which first appears in the *Theses on Feuerbach*, that the 'essence of man' has no concrete meaning except as designating the ensemble of social relations at a given time and in a given society. How can these two claims be reconciled? The answer lies in recognizing that a condition of human nature (in its normative as distinguished from its purely biological sense) has not, for Marx, had realized in any past or present society, and that therefore any detailed elaboration, by someone living in Marx's time, of a future society in which the members' full potentialities were utilized would necessarily be highly speculative and not very serviceable.

The notion of a condition in which there occurs full utilization of human potentialities must be considered, like the notion of a realm of freedom with which it is synonymous, the key to the vision of a future socialist society that lies behind all Marx's writings. But it is an intrinsically elusive notion—not meaningless, but highly elusive. In addition to problems stemming from its having to do with a social condition that, in Marx's view, is as yet unrealized, this notion also has the peculiarity of referring to temporally changeable, rather than fixed, phenomena. In other words, Marx's denial that there exists a single, unique human essence applies to the future as well as to the past: the concrete meaning of a 'full realization of human potentialities' will always differ from one period to another, since these potentialities will themselves change in accordance with changes in technological and other historical conditions.

We can now see why Marx, in his capacity as theorist, was not given to elaborating Five- or Ten- or Hundred-Year Plans. Any state of affairs that he might possibly sketch in outline and label as desirable could not, in principle, be anything more than a 'transitional period'; yet the danger of its being treated as a Marxian utopia, or ultimate goal, would remain very great. His 1844 manuscript on 'Private Property and Communism' ends with the statement, '*Communism* is the necessary form and dynamic principle of the immediate future but not as such the goal of human development—the form of human society.' This has puzzled some interpreters; it should not have, given the tightrope of paradox that Marx is constrained to walk in his treatment of normative questions. Marx's 'vision of a possible future' is not really a set 'vision' at all, if by this is meant a single state of affairs capable of being mentally pictured and verbally delineated. How could it be such a state of affairs, if the expression 'realm of freedom' (implying, as it does, the existence of a wide range of choices for the members of society in determining their own destinies) is to be taken at face value? Within the terms of his own conceptual framework, Marx can only point in the direction of this 'realm of freedom'; he cannot inform us what it will be like.

The preceding considerations raise serious questions about another concept that has usually been taken to be at the heart of Marx's philosophy in its normative aspect—namely, that of 'the revolution'. The frequent use of the definite article, 'the', in references to this concept serves to reinforce the assumption that a single, quasi-apocalyptic event is being envisaged. But this manner of conceiving it presupposes a degree of rigidity in the goal sought by the participants in 'the revolution' that does not square with Marx's approach to such a goal. In fact, Marx himself seldom writes in an apocalyptic fashion about the envisaged fundamental social change from capitalism to his 'society of associated producers'. At the same time, however, he preserves the idea that this change would be relatively fundamental, not just causal or 'incremental'. But many followers of his have failed to maintain Marx's delicate balance on this issue; their theories have run the gamut from the extremely apocalyptic to the merely reformist, the latter epitomized in Eduard Bernstein's famous dictum that 'the movement means everything for me and . . . what is *usually* called "the final aim of socialism" is nothing'. For Marx, the final aim is not 'nothing', but is is unspecifiable in a fixed way. Consequently, 'the revolution' must itself be seen as an open-ended and, with respect to the future, temporally unbounded concept within Marx's philosophy; some later Marxists have spoken, though with a wide range of exact meanings in mind, of its having to be 'permanent'. In any case, any political take-over by individuals sympathetic to Marxism could at best be only the beginning of the sort of fundamental social change that he had in mind.

If Marx is not, as we have seen, able to draw up blueprints for his vision of a possible future, then what can he say about it? A great deal. The philosophy of Marx, I have argued throughout this book, is above all a *critical* philosophy, furnishing a methodology for conceiving of existing social structures as transitory and subject to supersession, and offering descriptive generalizations about these structures and about past history with a view to, among other things, rendering the possibility of such supersession more plausible. To understand the normative aspect of Marx's thought is, above all, to become familiar with those features of present-day society that he regards as most restrictive of the free exercise and development of the potentialities of society's members. Thus the normative and the descriptive are inextricably interconnected in the philosophy of Marx, even though he does not pretend to deduce 'is's' from 'oughts'.

There are a number of ways, differing in connotation but conceptually interrelated, in which Marx designates these restrictive features. 'Alienation' is the most familiar. This term is often understood nowadays in a primarily psychological sense, but this sense, while it is not wholly uncongenial to Marx, is not the one in which he is most interested. When he speaks of 'alienation', he means above all a social state of affairs in which the products of an individual's labour, and hence also that labour itself (and, in general, what Marx calls one's 'life-activities'), are made to serve purposes that run counter to the full development of his or her potentialities. At the root of this state of affairs lie, according to Marx, the enforced division of labour and the institution of private property, which manifest themselves in the fact of society's being torn between dominant and subordinate social classes. Another way of designating this state, one that we have previously considered, is to say that it is one in which many human needs go unmet. Common to all these descriptions is the idea of restriction, of limitation, of—to use a dialectical term as dear to Marx as it was to Hegel— negation. The elimination of these conditions, unspecifiable in a positive sense but nevertheless comprehensible as a radical social change, is what Marx sometimes calls 'the negation of the negation'. This is perhaps the most general possible description of Marx's social vision.

The various passages, spanning the course of his career, in which Marx alludes to this vision are all efforts at restating this same theme. The notorious allusion to hunting, fishing, cattle-raising, and criticizing, in *The German Ideology*, is an obvious instance of such restatement: the first three activities are commonly regarded as among the earliest serious occupations of humanity, while the fourth is taken by Marx to typify the activity of the modern German intellectual. (This last, of course, is Marx's principal activity too, although he wishes to distinguish sharply between the practical thrust of his sort of criticism and the purely theoretical orientation

of most of his contemporaries.) The point, for Marx, is the removal
of the stultifying effects of an enforced division of labour. Similarly,
Marx's repetition of the slogan, '. . . to each according to his
needs!', is misunderstood if it is taken as a proposal for a rival Marxian theory of justice, alleged to be better than other such theories;
rather, it is another expression of his vision of a society freed from,
or more accurately in the process of freeing itself from, the restraints
on the development of human possibilities that characterize the present. Marx assumes that, given the limitations of human beings as
isolated individuals, the society of his vision will be characterized
by considerable mutual co-operation, but he does not attempt to
specify in detail the nature of such new, associative social structures.

At the apex of many of the most restrictive elements in contemporary society is, as Marx sees it, the Leviathan, the modern
State apotheosized by Hegel. The State, or government, holds
class-divided society together, supporting the existing relationships
of dominance and subordination, while acting to suppress or,
better yet, forestall manifestations of antagonism by the subordinate
class(es). In a classless society, this key function of the modern
State would be obviated; Marx imagines that other functions of the
State would similarly fall, gradually, into disuse, while still useful
public services would be assumed by non-political agencies. This
necessarily complex possible future process, the details of which can
only be treated in a very speculative way, is what Engels calls 'the
withering away of the state'. Marx says much less about it than
Engels does, but he accepts the same general scheme. It is fair to
say, therefore, that an important element in Marx's long-range
future vision is an anarchistic one (in the literal sense of a govern-
ment-less society), however much Marx came to oppose the
organized anarchist movement that rose to prominence during his
lifetime.

Most salient among the state-connected institutions that Marx regards as superfluous in a possible future 'post-political' society is
law. He contends that law as we know it in our society articulates
and enforces patterns of dominance and subordination and of
restraint. It will be recalled that typically, according to him,
theories of justice justify restrictive legal systems, whether actual or
proposed. To the degree to which this is true, it follows that the
abolition of legal systems of a traditional sort would render traditional theories of justice equally superfluous. It is no very great leap

from speaking of this eventuality to speaking of a possible future time when theories of morality in general would exist only as historical curiosities. And so we return, by way of this chain of thought, to the Marxian conception of moral philosophy as a dispensable enterprise. In his own generally (not, to be sure, always) non-moralistic manner of writing about ethical issues, as we have seen, Marx endeavours to anticipate and illustrate the process of dispensing with ethics that he expects to become widespread in the future, as the members of society gradually cease either thinking or needing to think primarily in terms of limiting one another's ranges of conduct and begin to expand practices of co-operation, to mutual advantage.

Although it is virtually impossible to maintain that Marx's treatment of this vast and deliberately under-developed aspect of his thought is adequate to the issues, I find the procedure of extending ideas of radical social change to their conceptual limits, as Marx does when he writes, for instance, about the supersession of states, legal systems, and moralities, to be an interesting and worthwhile mental exercise. But it is the sort of exercise that generates more than the usual number of serious doubts about validity. For example, can positive, mutually supportive behaviour patterns among members of a social 'realm of freedom' ever possibly become so pervasive as to eliminate all need for what is now called 'criminal law', or will not certain psychological incentives to negative conduct, such as sadism, always remain *at least as possibilities* in any future society? Or again, if we accept the commonplace definition of law as certain kinds of social rules, is it meaningful to think of proceeding even beyond the abolition of legal systems as we now know them to the abolition of a broader spectrum of social rules? Can there, alternatively, be whole systems of social rules that are completely devoid of the restrictive, inhibiting function attributed by Marx to contemporary legal systems?

To indulge in such speculations is at once to engage in fascinating mental play and to understand better than before why Marx, who was both extremely radical in his vision of a possible future and very serious about wishing to see it begin to be realized as soon as possible, wrote so little about it. He feared, no doubt with very good reason, that he might come to be regarded as a wild-eyed utopian and hence either lose influence over the course of events in the workers' movements of his time, or else be misunderstood concerning the social change that he regarded as *immediately* feasible. These fears were reinforced by the success of Bakunin's anarchists, whose ideas Marx considered deficient by the standard of feasibility, within the International during a portion of Marx's later years.

For Marx had, above all else with respect to his vision of a possible future, a very healthy regard for considerations of what was feasible and what unfeasible, whether in his own time or at any future time. As he said in his *Critique of the Gotha Programme*, apropos of the envisaged 'transition period' to a 'higher phase' of society,

What we have to deal with here is a communist society, not as it has *developed* on its own foundations, but, on the contrary, as it *emerges* from capitalist society; which is thus in every aspect, economically, morally, and intellectually, still stamped with the birthmarks of the old society from whose womb it emerges. (*Critique of the Gotha Programme*, Vol. 1, Section 3.)

Never having the opportunity to lead a successful political revolution, and hence to deal with immediate problems of social organization, Marx was never obliged to draw up a detailed programme of the sort that Lenin, for instance, was required to prepare. Marx always insisted that any such programme would have to be tailored to the particular circumstances of time and place, even though certain policies would be generally applicable in all the European countries of his day. In keeping with this, in *The Communist Manifesto* he listed ten such generally applicable policies, several of them (e.g., free public education and the abolition of then current child labour practices) not radical at all by twentieth-century standards, others (e.g., the nationalization of certain industries, such as transport, but not of all) both somewhat more radical and yet, in retrospect, curiously qualified. (The remaining policies, in essence, are: abolition of landed property and of inheritance rights, establishment of a heavy progressive income tax, confiscation of emigrants' property, creation of a State bank, expansion of land cultivation, insistence on equal universal liability to labour, creation of 'industrial armies', especially for agriculture, and gradual elimination of the gap between town and country, manufacturing and agriculture.) These proposals, it should be stressed, are clearly secondary to the principal message of the *Manifesto*; they are intended as practical suggestions for the near future, rather than as hard-core theory.

In short, Marx's radical, open-ended vision of a realm of freedom serves to orient his entire thought, but it does not distract him from engaging in the often excruciatingly detailed critical analysis of existing social structures that he regarded as his principal theoretical task. He recognized that intoxication with the heady but, in the end, hopelessly vague idea of a totally free society might get in the way of taking first steps towards the abolition of certain specific present-day restrictions on freedom that could, realistically speaking, be abolished. That is why, as we have seen, Marx inserts his warning that a modicum of necessary labour will always remain, in any imaginable future society, into his stirring paragraph about the realm of freedom near the end of *Capital*, and why he—paradoxically, at first glance—terminates that paragraph with the sober, indisputably commonsense suggestion that the shortening of the working day would be a reasonable first step.

8 Other Marxisms

The title of this final chapter cannot but be controversial, no matter what it is; the same holds for the choice of material in it. Some will deny that certain theorists whom I am about to mention are Marxist at all; some will object to my use of the adjective 'other' in the title, maintaining that one or another of these theorists is simply following in Marx's path, not blazing a new one. And, of course, my omissions of names deemed by many to be more significant than those selected will be deplored.

The present chapter is, perforce, incomplete and sketchy. My choice of the theorists who, in the second half of it, will receive more than a passing mention—namely, Lenin, Lukács, Sartre, Althusser, and members of the so-called 'Praxis group' of Yugoslavia—has been dictated by considerations of their philosophical interest, diversity, and relative novelty, in the sense of their dealing with issues left comparatively untouched by Marx himself. Historical importance has been of lesser concern to me, although it can surely not be entirely disregarded in my choices, particularly of Lenin and of the Yugoslavians.

Were I to undertake at this point an intellectual history of the Marxist tradition since Marx's death, there are certain additional figures whom I would feel bound to consider. I shall now proceed to mention them, following a rough chronological sequence until I come to the period after the Second World War. First in order, curiously enough, would be Engels, to whom I have already devoted special attention under the rubric of 'Philosophical Influences' on Marx's thought, in Chapter 2. It is a significant fact that Engels survived his colleague by more than a decade, during which time he continued to publish cogent popularizations of Marx's thought and to engage in copious correspondence, in addition to completing the editing of *Capital*. I have indicated, throughout the course of the present book, some of the important differences in emphasis and perhaps even in substance that can be discovered to exist between Engels's Marxism and Marx's; certain of these differences have unquestionably had profound effects on both the intellectual and the political history of the world in the past century.

Among the theorists, besides Lenin, with whom the intellectual historian would be compelled to deal from the period beginning immediately before Engels's death and lasting until some twenty years thereafter, Georgi Plekhanov, Karl Kautsky, Eduard Bernstein, and Rosa Luxemburg would certainly have to be included. Plekhanov cared about fundamental philosophical issues, especially those of determinism and of the relationship between the individual and the group in a Marxist philosophy of history; but his resolutions of them are wooden and somewhat deficient in subtlety. Kautsky continued Engels's work of popularization and did so fairly adequately, but he contributed very little that was new to Marxist philosophy. Like Engels, he was extremely sceptical of the entire non-Marxist philosophical tradition (in particular the Hegelian heritage), but he was also considerably less adept in it, and less well informed about it, than was his predecessor. The circumstance had considerable influence on the development of the German Social Democratic Party, over the enormous membership of which Kautsky's theoretical leadership was great and comparatively long-lived.

Bernstein, frequently denounced by Social Democratic Party opponents as the first great 'revisionist', probably deserves that epithet (whether one prefers to employ it with horror, with gratitude, or with indifference), among others. It is to Bernstein's credit as a political figure that he withstood the ultra-nationalist tide that engulfed so many German socialists on the eve of the 'Great War', but there is little with which one can credit him as a philosopher. Among his salient conclusions was the view that Marxism could afford to dispense with dialectical methodology. In the previous chapter, I noted Bernstein's even better-known pronouncement that the movement of socialism, as distinguished from whatever might be considered its goal, was all that mattered. By comparison, Rosa Luxemburg's writings reveal a subtle and first-rate thinker, but her best work lies in economic and political areas with which we have been only peripherally concerned in this book. Her *The Accumulation of Capital*, in which she constructively criticizes Marx's theory of capitalist reproduction and develops significant insights into the complex phenomenon of imperialism, stands alone, or nearly so, among works in economic theory that exude an intellectual atmosphere comparable to that of *Capital* itself (i.e., a breadth of knowledge in numerous domains and a sense of comprehensiveness or 'totality').

György Lukács published his epochal *History and Class Consciousness* in 1923. I shall devote special attention to this book, even though Lukács later insisted on its inadequacies and wrote many other books, because of its peculiar intellectual audacity; in addition, its influence over a later generation of French philosophers, including Sartre, was, by their own admission, considerable. Another significant philosopher within the Marxist tradition who emerged contemporaneously with Lukács was Karl Korsch; his *Marxism and Philosophy* did much to set the historical record straight for a generation weaned on Kautsky, but his insistence on maintaining a critical stance towards 'orthodox' Marxist political leaderships, both German and Soviet, resulted in his being widely treated as a pariah. Korsch's contribution was less one of adding new elements to Marxism than of recalling what most so-called Marxists of the time had forgotten. As a consequence, he will not be accorded an extended treatment here.

Another towering figure most properly identified with the decade of the 1920s is Antonio Gramsci. Long an important organizer and journalist within the nascent Italian Communist Party, he wrote some of his most perceptive essays while imprisoned by the regime of Benito Mussolini. Gramsci's most innovative work lay in analysing cultural factors—art, literature, life-styles, etc.—as significant phenomena for a more adequate and comprehensive criticism of existing social structures than that provided by Marx himself; it was the culture of his own Italy, of course, to which Gramsci devoted the greatest attention. Finally, the 1920s in the Soviet Union witnessed a brief period of significant philosophical work, particularly in the field of the philosophy of law. Reysner and Pashukanis are probably the foremost of a group of thinkers who dealt with such questions as the status of national and international legal systems both in a future socialist society and during a period of transition of the sort in which they considered themselves to be.

It is noteworthy that the climate of often fruitful discussion about law within a Marxist framework gave way, during the 1930s in the Soviet Union, to the authority of Andrei Vyshinsky in this field. Vyshinsky was the Procurator of the USSR during the infamous Moscow Purge Trials. The systematic political repression of which these trials were the most illustrious examples paralleled a repression of theoretical inquiry that resulted in the elevation of exceedingly mediocre tracts by members of the Soviet Communist Party leadership, notably Stalin himself, to positions of highest esteem within that country and among many of its foreign admirers. This state of affairs persisted for many years. When, for example, a short statement by Stalin (in 1950) on the social role of language was published, there occurred throughout the country an overnight abandonment of the theories of N. Y. Marr, the linguist previously held in highest regard by Soviet scholars; it was enough that Stalin had dissented from Marr's view (that language was a purely 'superstructural' phenomenon, not at all a part of a society's material 'base').

If one attempts as an intellectual historian to survey writings ostensibly composed from within the Marxist tradition in the 1930s with a view to discovering significant new contributions, one may well draw a very paradoxical conclusion: amid much that is bleak, much that is repetitious, and relatively little that is fresh, one name that stands out is that of an avowed admirer of Stalin's, whose own familiarity with the Western philosophical tradition out of which Marx emerged was necessarily very superficial. I am referring to Mao Tse-tung, several of whose most important theoretical statements, such as his treatise 'On practice', date from the second half of that decade. It is impossible honestly to apply the usual canons of Western philosophical criticism, to some of which even Lenin, despite his early contempt for traditional academic philosophy, adhered, to the thought of Mao. I shall not attempt to do so. Nevertheless, it is important to acknowledge his role as a very thoughtful innovator with respect to Marxist theory. Mao's insistence, for instance, on writing philosophy in a terminology that should be intelligible to the ordinary member of Chinese society itself points to a very different conception of theory from that held by Marx, while at the same time it appears consistent with certain tendencies implicit in Marx's ideas about joining theory with practice.

In the years immediately following the Second World War and continuing up to the present time, diversity of orientations among followers of Marx has become increasingly commonplace. A major factor, in addition to the obvious political and social developments, in bringing this about was the widespread dissemination of Marx's *1844 Manuscripts* in Western countries during the late 1940s, the 1950s and the early 1960s. In France, intensive new interest in Marxist thought on the part of philosophers with already established reputations as existential phenomenologists, notably Jean-Paul Sartre, Maurice Merleau-Ponty, and Simone de Beauvoir, began to be manifested in the immediate aftermath of the German occupation. Their Marxisms, heavily influenced by their background knowledge of Hegel and the similarities between their own philosophical concerns about ethical questions and those exhibited in Marx's earlier, and hitherto less well known, writings, clashed markedly with the Marxisms of their more 'orthodox' contemporaries. The names of Roger Garaudy and of the sociologist-philosopher Henri Lefebvre stand out among the latter; both of them have themselves gone their separate ways, particularly after their enforced separations (at different times, and for different reasons) from the Communist Party in the thirty years since the war. Lefebvre's detailed work on the subject of Marxism as a critique of the structures of 'everyday life' is especially interesting. The first important publications of Louis Althusser, to whom I shall return later in this chapter, date from a more recent time than do those of the above-mentioned individuals.

In Germany, probably the most important original contributor to Marxist thought during the post-war period has been Ernst Bloch. Bloch's contributions can hardly, to be sure, be restricted to a mere three decades, since his *Spirit of Utopia* was published before 1920, and his study of the early German religious revolutionary Thomas Münzer first appeared in 1921. But Bloch's most central work, *The Principle of Hope*, was written during his exile in the United States from 1938 to 1947. His perennial theme has been that Marxist thought is the culmination, and points towards the practical fulfilment, of centuries of utopian thinking in philosophy, theology, and other areas of culture. A resident first of East and then of West Germany after his return from the United States, Bloch has generated less of a personal following among students of philosophy than have many other German figures of comparable stature (such as the existentialist thinker, Martin Heidegger, to whose concept of 'dread' and related interpretative categories of human existence Bloch has attempted to counterpose his Marxist theory of 'hope'); but Bloch's notoriety is likely to increase in the coming years, particularly as more of his desperately difficult prose becomes available in, as one may hope, lucid English translations.

The other major German developments in philosophy and sociology that owe considerable debts to Marx have emanated from a group of individuals who became colleagues during the 1920s and

F

1930s and are known, collectively, as the 'Frankfurt School'. What characterized all, or most, of the original members of this group, in addition to their interest in exploring questions raised by Marx from a perspective outside that of Communist Party orthodoxy, was a strong sense, so underdeveloped in the philosophy of Marx himself, of the importance of psychological factors in determining social structures and events. Among the most interesting members of this group are the literary critic, Walter Benjamin, who died in 1940, the philosopher and social psychologist, Theodor Adorno, and Herbert Marcuse, whose pessimistic analyses of industrialized Western societies and optimistic projections of the expanded possibilities for psychological gratification and aesthetic creativity in a non-repressive society of the future, exerted a considerable influence over leaders of student protest movements in various countries during the latter half of the 1960s.

A later generation of individuals with some historical ties to the original Frankfurt group is exerting considerable influence over contemporary German thought; Jürgen Habermas is most prominent among them. Habermas is concerned to examine the role of human interests, including the so-called 'cognitive interest', in predetermining the content particularly of the sciences and technology; he has also come increasingly to focus on the function of language in determining social structures. Habermas's philosophy is an interesting example of the integration of Marxism with numerous other thought currents, to a point at which it becomes quite arbitrary to decide whether to classify the new set of ideas as a Marxism or not. This process of integration is not yet as far advanced in the English-speaking countries, but it seems most likely eventually to become so. This kind of development will greatly complicate the task of the intellectual historian of the future.

Finally, brief mention must be made of the outpouring of interesting philosophical work in Eastern Europe that dates roughly from the period of the so-called 'thaw', which began with Nikita Khrushchev's denunciation of Stalinism (Yugoslavia, to be considered later, is a special case; there the philosophical renascence began earlier). In Poland, the controversy between Adam Schaff, at the time an official theoretician, but one gifted with greater philosophical acumen than most of those who hold similar positions, and Leszek Kolakowski, particularly on the subject of Marxism and ethics, was lively and interesting. Within a few years, however, as a result largely of his political stance, Kolakowski was constrained to leave the country. In Hungary, despite the atmosphere of recrimination that followed the Budapest uprising, a certain flowering of inquiry among a handful of younger philosophers occurred in the early 1960s; the name of Agnes Heller is perhaps the best known of this group. But political conditions since the invasion of Czechoslovakia by other Warsaw Pact countries in 1968 have adversely affected the research and productivity of these Hungarian thinkers. In Czechoslovakia itself the effects have been even starker. Karl Košik's important *Dialectics of the Concrete* is a testimonial to a past era of openness and intellectual exploration in that country. Perhaps such an atmosphere will be restored, in Czechoslovakia and elsewhere in Eastern Europe, in the near future. Perhaps an optimist could detect signs of such a restoration even now. But the present state of affairs leaves a great deal to be desired.

Having now indicated a few of the main currents in the nearly one-hundred-year odyssey of Marxist thinking from Marx's death to the present, I wish, in the remainder of this chapter, to take a somewhat closer look at the five 'other Marxisms' that I listed earlier. Lenin's is the first.

(a) Lenin

In Chapter 4, I devoted considerable attention to a critique of Lenin's conceptions of 'matter' and of 'materialism' and to his reflection theory of cognition. I do not now propose to retrace these steps. *Materialism and Empiro-Criticism*, the locus of these discussions by Lenin, is, I have suggested, a work of inferior intellectual quality, much more noteworthy for the enthusiasm of its author's polemical thrusts than for carefulness in considering the issues. (To be fair to Lenin, it was precisely the polemical purpose that was uppermost in his own mind, since he regarded the new wave of interest in what we can retrospectively label, broadly speaking, neo-Kantian theories of knowledge as a threat to the growth of adherence to Marxism among Russian intellectuals, and perhaps he was right about this.) This book stands as Lenin's one important contribution to questions that philosophers have traditionally considered most fundamental: the nature of reality and the nature of knowledge. However, Lenin has ideas of considerable philosophical interest to offer concerning two related matters about which he wrote voluminously and with much greater authority—namely, the role of the revolutionary party in effecting fundamental social change and the future of the State.

Marx, although throughout most of his life active in radical political organizations, never set store by the notion of bringing about fundamental social change through the efforts of a (relatively) small, conspiratorial band of professional revolutionaries. In fact, as we have seen, he said very little about the mechanisms whereby a transition to socialism might be expected to take place. Lenin, on the other hand, regarded the professional revolutionary organization as a practical necessity in light of the repressive political conditions in Russia, and he held very explicit views about the mechanisms of change.

Lenin had less confidence about the likely course of future events than did Marx. This is paradoxical, in view of Lenin's historical responsibility for the tradition of rigid 'orthodoxy', generally committed to an image of itself as the repository of necessary social scientific laws, that has characterized Soviet Marxism. He feared a reliance on 'spontaneity', as he called it—the decisions and activities of ordinary workers, unguided by a specially trained leadership. He foresaw, much better than had Marx, the possibilities for diverting members of the proletariat from revolutionary activities; indeed, in the history of the mainstream of the German Social Democratic Party during his own lifetime, Lenin thought he discerned the realization of some of those possibilities. His solution to this danger, as he saw it, was to stress the importance of 'consciousness'—that is, the active co-ordination and direction of the workers' movement by their 'vanguard' party.

What is most striking about this, from a philosophical point of view, is the conceptual linkage that can be discerned between this Leninist justification of the strong, tightly organized party and his theory of knowledge. One of the greatest obstacles to the workers' attainment of full 'revolutionary consciousness', according to Lenin, in addition to the legal prohibitions against their organizing, is the material limitations imposed on them by demanding working hours. How is it physically possible for the ordinary person, constantly driven to the verge of exhaustion by long and demanding working hours, to achieve an accurate and comprehensive knowledge of the state of his society, the 'reflection' of objective reality of which Lenin speaks? Time and effort are required in order to acquire such knowledge and then to act upon it; people whose careers consist in agitational and revolutionary activity are able to devote the needed time and effort. If the truth about society is of the straightforward, objective sort that Lenin conceives it to be, and if the party members are genuinely dedicated and have set aside considerations of self-interest, then it seems highly unlikely that the collective wisdom of these individuals, implemented through the procedure that Lenin called 'democratic centralism' (open discussion of issues and options before arriving at a decision, universal adherence to a decision once made), would be misguided. And so the seeds have been sown, through this reasoning process, for the view that the Party is nearly infallible in its political judgements.

But if the Communist Party is guaranteed in advance, so to speak, to be so beneficial to the cause of social progress prior to its seizure of political power, then there would appear to be little urgency in working towards its dissolution after a successful political revolution. Rule by the party—in the interests, of course, of the masses of workers and peasants—is Lenin's concrete application of Marx's idea of a transitional period of 'dictatorship of the proletariat'. Some of the later variations on this theme, introduced by Stalin and his successors and imitators, are of course not directly attributable either to Lenin's policies or to his philosophy; but it is noteworthy that, in his famous *State and Revolution*—a work that was interrupted and left incomplete by the onset of the events that led to his seizure of power—Lenin indicates more clearly than Marx ever did that he expects the transitional period to be a lengthy one.

One of the constant themes throughout *State and Revolution* is that of coercion. The very term 'dictatorship' implies the use of force, as Lenin stresses, and he is highly sceptical about the possibility of there occurring an overnight change in individuals' social behaviour as a result of radical changes in social structures. Hence, there will be a need for 'factory discipline', as he calls it, and this discipline will need largely to be imposed until such time as the new ways of conduct become habitual with the population. In short, Lenin was a strong believer in what contemporary psychologists call behaviour modification. Although it would be very false to claim that Lenin lacked all sense of vision of a radically different future society (there is even a passage in his *What Is To Be Done?* in which he indulges in a sort of reverie on the theme 'We ought to dream!'), his approach to questions about the future, concerning which he naturally wrote a great deal more than Marx himself, places much more stress on immediate and short-term strategies. Within this perspective, Marx's long-range commitment to a restraint-free society is of far less importance.

Indeed, we may ask ourselves whether this latter conception of Marx's is ultimately compatible with Lenin's vision of a thoroughly habituated society, in which the overt coercions of the transitional period have been internalized. Lenin had no doubt that it was. He also believed that the insistence on such quasi-ideological notions as that of 'communist morality' was justifiable, within a Marxist conceptual framework, at a time when powerful individuals throughout the world remained hostile to his new order. A certain simplification of Marx's more critical theory of ideology was the inevitable result of this belief. Concerning most matters, Lenin was able to cite Marxian-Engelsian texts in profusion, and he did not appear to be intent on distorting the spirit of the original thought. Yet he unquestionably did alter it—whether constructively or destructively, it is for the student to decide—and thus it is no accident that his most faithful intellectual heirs refer so frequently to 'Marxist-Leninist ideology', rather than to the thought of Marx by itself.

(b) Lukács

Before Marx's early manuscripts had been brought to light, the German-educated Hungarian, György Lukács, succeeded in divining some of the historical linkages between Marx's thought and Hegel's that the manuscripts themselves subsequently verified. Lukács placed Marx squarely within the Hegelian tradition. In fact, as he himself later admitted, Lukács carried this association to excess, so that, while he of course never explicitly endorsed a philosophical stance of idealism, in any of its many interrelated senses, the Hegel-steeped version of Marxism that he developed in *History and Class Consciousness* has strongly idealistic overtones. Let us consider this.

A single theme, even a single term, dominates the greater part of *History and Class Consciousness*: the term is 'reification'. Literally, of course, the term means the process of 'thing-making'; when applied to acts of consciousness, as it is intended by Lukács to be, it means filling one's conceptual space with thing-like objects, and hence, imparting fixedness or rigidity to one's view of the world. According to Lukács, pre-proletarian class ways of thinking, in particular those of the bourgeoisie, are characterized above all by reifications; the whole of Hegel's system, despite Hegel's own identification with the interests of the bourgeois class, demonstrates this. Bourgeois thought elevates 'objective' facts and calculative reasoning to positions of supreme importance, and yet at the same time—as one sees, for instance, in the philosophy of Kant—it glorifies the role of the individual (human) subject. Hence, it has failed to solve classical modern philosophy's dichotomy between subject and object, and instead oscillates constantly between crude empiricism and an abstract utopianism that verges on irrationality. (In his much later work, *The Destruction of Reason*, Lukács treats Nazism as one outcome of this historical oscillation of bourgeois thought.) The reifying consciousness, by virtue of its incapacity to reach a resolution of its contradictory tendencies, is characterized above all by alienation.

By contrast, for Lukács, proletarian class-consciousness overcomes the historical dichotomy of subject and object. It is that way of thinking which rejects all reification, every tendency to allow one's conceptual structures to become thing-like and inflexible. Typical of this alternative way of thinking is Marx's rejection of the claims to unsurpassability made on behalf of the market system of commodity exchange by the bourgeois political economists. In his Afterword to the second German edition of *Capital,* after all, Marx had defended his retention of dialectical methodology primarily on the grounds of its enabling him more easily to discredit such claims.

In identifying proletarian class-consciousness with anti-reificatory unalienated thinking, however, Lukács carries to a breaking-point the problem about the exact identity of the proletarian class that I first noted in Chapter 1. For he is as aware as anyone else that vast numbers of actual industrial workers fail most of the time to think in the radical, dialectical fashion that he has ascribed to the class-consciousness of the proletariat. He is resolute and straightforward in his approach to this apparent problem. There is a difference, he readily acknowledges, between the ideal and the empirical consciousnesses of the proletariat, and it is in the former that he is primarily interested. (He owes a debt at this point to the theoretical conception of the 'ideal-type' developed for sociology by Max Weber, an important early influence on him.) Naturally, given this account of the actual state of affairs, a mediating agent is required to lead more workers in the direction of adopting the ideal proletarian class-consciousness as their own, and that mediator, Lukács maintains, is the Communist Party. Thus, starting from a conceptual framework and especially from a theory of knowledge at wide variance with Lenin's (particularly if we consider only the latter's early years), Lukács arrives at a very similar view of the Party; it should be no surprise, then, that he was a great admirer of Lenin's political thought.

In the 1930s, an exile from both Hungary and Germany, Lukács lived in Moscow and formally repudiated *History and Class Consciousness*. Was this action simply, as many observers claimed, a modern version of the story of Galileo, in which a strong secular Papacy forced a perceived heretic to renounce his still firmly held beliefs as the price for permitting him to engage in some further intellectual activity? Partly yes, and mostly no, Lukács seems to be saying in his cautious Preface to the new edition of the book in 1967. He makes a strong case for his having truly come to believe, in large part as a result of his first reading of Marx's just-deciphered 1844 manuscripts in 1930, that he had, in *History and Class Consciousness*, made a fundamental conceptual error: namely, he had identified alienation with objectification. Marx, on the contrary, in pointing in his early writings to the possible future development of a society in which the varieties of alienation that he enumerated had been overcome, had claimed that human beings in such a society would be able to regard and to treat each other as material objects without there following the invidious, restrictive consequences that are today associated with the notion of 'treating others as objects'.

Lukács admits to having phrased his early self-criticism in the exaggerated language that was demanded by Stalinist political authorities, but he regards the core of this self-criticism as correct. He also acknowledges, in his recent Preface (written just a few years before his death), the historical importance of *History and Class Consciousness*—an acknowledgement that would have been impossible in the period prior to the Second World War. Both of these points are important and, I think, difficult to dispute. If one identifies objectification with alienation, as Lukács did in his classic work, then, assuming that a mutually acceptable meaning of the vague term 'objectification' can be found, one is left with two alternatives, neither of them acceptable within the framework of Marx's thought. Either one admits, with Hegel, that the phenomenon of alienation is ineradicable in the social world (Hegel's overcoming of alienation in his realm of 'Absolute Spirit' is irrelevant here), or else one is left with a wildly utopian view of the ideal consciousness of the proletariat, one which, if it is not totally inconceivable, makes some sense only within an ethereal realm of pure thought from which most of the mundane facts of everyday human existence have been abstracted. Yet, Lukács's extreme formulation of the ideal-typical proletarian class-consciousness (together with, though to a lesser extent, his ideal-typical conception of the Communist Party) has played an important role, by virtue of its very extreme nature, in shaping discussions about alienation within a neo-Marxist context throughout the post-War period.

History and Class Consciousness is rich in many other themes besides the one that I have emphasized. For instance, Lukács insists on the category of 'totality' (comprehensiveness, a sense of the interrelatedness of disparate parts) as a central category for Marxism, by way of contrast with the piecemeal approach to social reality that is characteristic of non-dialectical thinkers; this marked another break with ways of thought typical of Social Democratic theorists in the period prior to the First World War, and it has also been taken up as an important concept by many subsequent writers. But what may well be most appreciated by later generations of readers of 'the early Lukács' is his talent for finding intriguing resemblances among apparently disparate forms of 'bourgeois' thought. In the English-speaking world, however, Lukács's principal influence up to the present time has been connected with his extensive writings in aesthetics and literary criticism, rather than with the theses contained in *History and Class Consciousness*, itself only recently translated into our language. His are probably the most sophisticated and informed formulations of the canons of 'socialist realism' as a perspective from which to evaluate works of art, particularly literary works. Although, like the philosophy of Marx itself, Lukács's ideas about aesthetics have sometimes been put to disreputable use by politicians intent on imposing narrow conformity on artists subject to their control, what Lukács has delineated as a positive aesthetic attitude is something quite different—a clear set of standards, but not a licence for intolerance. His list of significant 'realist' writers includes a number whose political affiliations were unquestionably non-Marxist. Indeed, Lukács's developed views on literature and art in general may be seen as a kind of compensation for the excessive exclusiveness and romanticism of his early theories about the proletariat and its party.

F*

(c) Sartre

One of the best known of twentieth-century Continental philosophers, Jean-Paul Sartre, had already established a reputation before World War II through both literary works and some short philosophical tracts, the latter primarily concerned with psychological phenomena (imagination, emotions, the nature of the self). At once an admirer of the 'phenomenological' method developed by Edmund Husserl and a dissenter from the turn towards idealism apparent in some of Husserl's later writings, Sartre achieved major recognition in 1943 with the publication of his massive, systematic treatise *Being and Nothingness*, sub-titled 'Essay in Phenomenological Ontology'. 'Existentialism', a label with which Sartre willingly associated his name, enjoyed a great vogue in the immediate post-War period; in the popular mind, it was, of course, more frequently associated with a loosely connected set of attitudes that characterized dramas and works of fiction by Sartre, Albert Camus, and others, than it was with the complex conceptual framework of *Being and Nothingness*. At the very height of this vogue, however, Sartre's own concerns were becoming increasingly political, and the history of Sartre's post-War intellectual development is primarily the history of the evolution of his variant of Marxism.

A relatively early essay, 'Materialism and Revolution' (1946), expresses commitment to the proletariat in its class-struggle, but it also stresses the 'mythical' character of materialism, as a set of metaphysical (to use the term as I have used it in this book) beliefs. Here Sartre anticipates the development of a pro-revolutionary philosophy that would replace the materialist 'myth'. His attacks on materialism have become somewhat muted in later years, as Sartre has become increasingly aware of meanings of the term that he is able to accept, but the spirit of dissatisfaction with the 'orthodox' Soviet version of Marxism that lay behind 'Materialism and Revolution' has remained. The most important writings for understanding Sartre's later thought (which he now prefers, I think mistakenly, not to label 'Marxist') are *Search for a Method* (1957) and *Critique of Dialectical Reason*, Volume I (1960), the published version of the latter containing the former as a preface. Most recently, Sartre has endeavoured to illustrate his Marx-inspired method of social inquiry in his formidable analysis of Gustave Flaubert, *The Family Idiot*, the three published volumes of which approximate to the three volumes of *Capital* in length.

The principal theme of *Search for a Method* is the need to elaborate a 'philosophical anthropology'—i.e., a set of categories and techniques for undertaking a systematic study of the species 'man', that would steer clear of the presuppositions (about human nature) of Freudianism, 'orthodox' Marxism, and Western behavioural social science. (Throughout his career, Sartre has forcefully combated the doctrine that there exists a fixed human nature.) In all these efforts to construct a 'science of man', Sartre detects a rigidity and, ultimately, a failure to account for those aspects of social events and history that depend upon individuals' free choices. Sartre's early reputation as an existentialist philosopher rested above all on his defence of a radical conception of human freedom; although he now concedes a great deal more reality than before to the forces of repression in society, his theoretical orientation in this regard remains fundamentally unchanged. The bases of individuals' choices themselves, according to Sartre, are in principle explainable through an understanding of their complex social preconditions, which differ somewhat in each case. But explanation will escape us if we neglect (as classical behaviourism is committed to doing) the internal perspective of the individual under study, or seek to impose vast, prefabricated categories on his or her actions, after the fashion of the French Communist Party journalists who 'knew', before any of the far more complicated facts of the situation became available to observers outside the country, that the Hungarian uprising of 1956 was simply a counter-revolutionary movement by remaining elements of the petite bourgeoisie. Sartre finds special support for his flexible approach in Marx's writings about historical events.

A secondary feature of *Search for a Method* is its treatment of intellectual history, especially the history of philosophy. Sartre accepts the Marxian view that there is a strong correlation between dominant philosophies of an era and the existing class divisions and material conditions, and he proceeds to provide a crude delineation of the major philosophical epochs since the time of Descartes. What is significant is that he declares the present era to be that of Marxism, and that he relegates the existentialist movement to the position of a marginal event, occasioned by the historically explainable blockage of Marxist 'orthodoxy' in what ought to have been a process of growth and development. 'Orthodox' Marxists failed to deal in creative ways with questions about the human individual that Marx had left unanswered; the success of existentialism, at least in its politically non-reactionary forms, is attributable to this. Sartre also contends, in a passage that has frequently been cited, that Marxism itself will give way to a new 'philosophy of freedom' once the present world-wide regime of scarcity has been replaced by one of comparative abundance; we, however, lack the intellectual capacity, he says, to imagine either that society or that philosophy.

Volume I of *The Critique of Dialectical Reason* is a monumental attempt to provide the beginnings of a 'Prolegomenon to Any Future Anthropology' that Sartre has declared, in *Search for a Method*, to be a great need of the present time. Although it exhibits a movement from its intentionally very abstract starting-points—namely, human beings regarded as being characterized by 'free *praxis*' acting upon inert matter in an effort to satisfy their basic needs under conditions of scarcity, to its more concrete terminal-point in a complex world of social institutions and classes, its level of abstractness in fact remains quite high throughout. Sartre's aim is to provide a general theory of fundamental social structures that might underpin Marx's more specific analyses of, in particular, capitalist society. It is not easy to decide whether the *Critique* would best be labelled 'sociology' or 'metaphysics' or something else. It is not, at any rate, intended as a universal theory about all reality, since at several points Sartre makes it clear that his theory is applicable only to human or humanoid beings living in a regime of scarcity.

The projected second volume of the *Critique*, which was to be, essentially, a philosophy of history based upon the results of Volume I, has been abandoned by Sartre; one reason that he gives for this is his comparative ignorance of non-Western histories and his incapacity, at his present age, to undertake an adequate study of them. But this situation makes inevitable a widespread dissatisfaction with Sartre's social philosophy; for it would have been in his developed theory of history (considered as an increasingly more global, integrated process of what Sartre calls 'totalization') that he would have had to come to grips with issues concerning the possibility of a future society radically different from present and past societies. As it is, the completed volume of the *Critique* leaves the reader sceptical about such a possibility. Sartre painstakingly describes, in his lengthy central section on the transition from a passive, alienation-suffused form of social organization that he calls 'seriality' to the active, self-directed form that he calls 'the group', the potential growth of unified revolutionary activity in social units of almost any size; but he then goes on at equally great length to examine the various ways in which even successful groups, once their initial goals have been attained, can become institutionalized and even bureaucratic, thus altering their characters once more in a direction of passivity. The latter development seems, in terms of Sartre's analysis, to be inevitable, or very nearly so. The obvious fact that Sartre has in mind the actual fate of social structures in the Soviet Union under Stalin and his successors as he elaborates his general analyses does nothing to alleviate his general tone of pessimism.

Some of Sartre's more 'orthodox' critics, such as Adam Schaff, have found greatest difficulty with his insistence on the ultimate reality of the individual as opposed to the social unit—his claim that the social unit is always 'constituted', never 'constitutive'. But I remain unconvinced that Sartre is essentially at odds with Marx on this point. Greater difficulties, it seems to me, are presented by two other facets of Sartre's thought: first, the apparent pessimism just referred to, together with his related failure to give criteria for assessing the overcoming of scarcity, and second, the ambiguity of his stance concerning materialism, along with his life-long reluctance to admit causality as a meaningful phenomenon within the conceptual framework of his philosophy. (Sartre's first criticisms of Descartes's metaphysical dualism date from the earliest years of his career, and yet, as nearly all his critics have noted, even the opposition between *praxis* and inorganic nature that is prominent in his *Critique* still bears some of the marks of the Cartesian position.)

At the same time, the new perspectives on Marx's philosophy that Sartre has provided—perspectives that have much to do with Sartre's strong interest in the meaning of 'man' and his comparatively weaker interest in economics— will both puzzle and stimulate students of that philosophy for years to come. His passionate sense of political commitment, his capacity for enormous syntheses, and his equally significant abhorrence of easy generalizations have combined to produce a more original and more comprehensive variant of Marxism than those of any of his contemporaries. His openness to data of all varieties and his opposition to the assumption of dogmatic metaphysical presuppositions, whether overt or concealed, in the interpretation of data constitute a more important Sartrean contribution to social theory than do most of the positive philosophical categories—*praxis*, 'group', etc.—for which he shows a preference in his *Critique of Dialectical Reason.*

(d) Althusser

Louis Althusser's Marx is a strong contrast with Sartre's. Althusser takes the stance of a philosophical (and political) 'hardliner'; the influence on him of the loosely defined 'structuralist' movement, associated at its origin with the anthropologist Claude Lévi-Strauss, has provided Althusser with additional methodological machinery from outside the Marxist tradition to support this stance. Marxism is first and foremost, for Althusser, a new science of history, the discovery of which he compares with the scientific revolutions of Galileo in physics and of Pythagoras in mathematics. The philosophical aspects of Marxism, though important (Althusser prides himself, for instance, on being one of the few to recognize Lenin as a philosopher, and a good one at that), are for Althusser clearly subordinate to its role as a positive science. Moreover, Althusser's own work is not highly systematic, even though he lays great stress on the systematic character of Marxist thought.

If the late 1950s and early 1960s were the period of widespread discovery of Marx's early writings, the mid-1960s witnessed a rediscovery of *Capital* and of Marx's other economic works; Althusser was in the forefront of this process of 'rediscovery'. What Althusser has found in the later Marx is someone who has effected a radical break with the Hegelian and humanist traditions of his younger years. This notion of an 'epistemological break' in Marx's development, combined with an insistence on the incomparably greater scientific value of the 'mature' writings that date from the period after the break, is the *leitmotif* of Althusser's version of Marxism.

'Humanism', for Althusser, is a non-scientific concept; 'socialism' is a scientific one. Talk of 'socialist humanism', then, involves a confusion. Althusser maintains, in rather clear opposition to what is implied by Marx and Engels in *The German Ideology* and elsewhere, that ideology, meaning non-scientific forms of systematic representations of the world, will continue to exist even in a communist society; it is to the domain of 'ideology' that he assigns the notion of 'humanism'. Thus he manages to find an excuse for the use of the term 'humanism' even by some Soviet writers (an important exercise for French Communist Party members), just as long as they do not take themselves to be engaging in rigorous, scientific theory on such occasions. The mature Marx, he is convinced, was a philosophical anti-humanist, who found the key to social scientific explanation in structures and relationships rather than in individuals' aspirations and actions.

A second important theme in Althusser's work is that of social 'over-determination'. Simplistic versions of Marxism would have it that social change is always explicable, in the last analysis, by a clash between two (and only two) incompatible ('contradictory') phenomena, and that this opposition is essentially an economic one, in the narrow sense of that word. Against such conceptions, Althusser maintains both that such pure oppositions are never to be found in reality, and that the practical contradictions that do exist in society are never, at any time, *purely* economic. The social world and history are complex; whatever economic opposition the scientific theory of Marxism may discern, at a given point in time, as being fundamental is always going to be 'over-determined'— that is, inextricably influenced by many other factors, such as political and cultural ones, in such a way that the 'basic' contradiction may frequently not even appear salient to the social actors.

Althusser is adept at drawing fine conceptual distinctions and at developing technical categories for Marxist interpretation. (Typical of this is his interesting division into 'Generalities I, II, and III'— the raw data, the component parts of the scientific theoretical framework that is employed at a given time, and the final, concrete scientific truths, respectively.) These categories are themselves, admittedly, often not to be found by name in Marx's writings, but this does not diminish Althusser's confidence in the greater orthodoxy of his Marxism by comparison particularly with Marx's recent 'humanist' interpreters. There is an excessive tone of dogmatism about his essays that serves as a contrast to his scholarly caution and his tendency to multiply qualifications. (For instance, in elaborating on the nature of Marx's alleged 'epistemological break', which has become so much of a watchword with Althusser's numerous followers, Althusser feels constrained to divide Marx's works into *four* distinct periods, rather than two, with the early period itself being subdivided again.) Moreover, his insistence on the extremely radical nature of the historical 'break' itself is certainly exaggerated, and his stress, at times reminiscent of the nineteenth-century positivism of Auguste Comte, on the 'scientific' character of the work of the 'mature Marx' relies for its effect on a number of undemonstrable beliefs about the meaning of 'science'.

On the other hand, Althusser's positive contributions to understanding Marx's philosophy have been numerous. His insistence on rigour, his high dedication to 'theoretical practice' as an important sort of labour, and his often cogent criticisms of those who might be tempted to reduce Marx to a sentimental humanist, all of whose philosophically important claims were presumably made before 1845, have helped raise the level of contemporary discussion.

(e) The Yugoslavs

The greatest group impetus, during the post-War period, to reconsidering Marxism as a humanistic world-view has emanated from the limited ranks of the professional philosophers of Yugoslavia. It is incorrect to think that all recent Yugoslav philosophy has been taught and written within the ambit of the so-called '*Praxis* group', and yet the editors and writers of the journal of that name have played the leading role in establishing the national philosophical reputation. It is even more mistaken to equate the theoretical positions of members of the '*Praxis* group' with the politics of the country's prevailing regime, for a campaign conducted by elements of that regime succeeded in bringing about the suspension of several eminent philosophers from their teaching positions and the cessation of publication of *Praxis* in 1975; nevertheless, it was the special history and character of the post-War Yugoslav Government that created the conditions for the philosophical developments to which I am referring.

Among the most prominent Yugoslav philosophers are Gajo Petrovič, Mihailo Marković, and Svetozar Stojanović. Of the three, Petrovič has been most heavily influenced by contemporary currents in Continental philosophy, such as the thought of Heidegger, whereas the other two have adopted certain techniques of recent British philosophy. These three and their colleagues, however, are all heterogeneous in their styles and special interests; what they have in common are a certain social situation and a certain theoretical orientation. I wish briefly to focus here on what is common.

Political events in the late 1940s resulted in the Yugoslav Government's decision to remove itself, in large measure, from the influence of the Soviet Government and to introduce new and somewhat different domestic institutional arrangements, in accordance with the principle of 'workers' self-management'. This constituted an attempt to deal in practical ways with some of the problems surrounding Marx's 'vision of a possible future', along lines other than those followed by the Soviet Union. The 'laboratory' in which this attempt was undertaken was far from ideal: a collection of neighbouring but historically, linguistically, and even ethnically diverse territories, welded together into a single political unit only in the present century, and characterized by intense rivalries and vastly disparate levels of economic well-being and industrial development. Perhaps the single major force for national unity in the immediate post-War period was a hero of the Partisan resistance movement, Marshal Tito—an individual rather than a set of shared purposes.

The philosophers who came to prominence in this situation all shared a certain commitment to the ideal of self-management as being more in keeping with their and Marx's visions than the strong direction 'from above' that has come to characterize Soviet industry and other aspects of everyday life in the Soviet Union. They found support for this position particularly in Marx's early writings, and much of their own work has been devoted to analysing the implications of what Marx says there about eliminating alienation and bringing about a freer social state of affairs. They have attacked as aberrant both the 'official' theory of the so-called 'orthodox' Marxists—the standardized 'dialectical materialism' that forms the content of required courses in so many academic institutions today —and the repressive police practices that are connected with the label 'Stalinism'.

At the same time, the thinkers in question have tried to take very seriously their role as philosophers in a society that is said to be 'on the road to socialism'. Marx clearly implied that, with the rise to power of the proletariat (or of some reasonable later fascimile of the proletariat of his own day), the status and nature of philosophy would necessarily change radically; as we have seen, however, he said almost nothing about what the practice of philosophy or of whatever sort of theoretical thinking might replace it, would become. The *Praxis* philosophers have engaged, along with their conceptual analyses of 'freedom', 'revolution', and so on, in critical studies of problems of their own society; they have exhibited, on the whole, great facility in moving back and forth between the highly theoretical and the immediately practical. They have admitted, and indeed have often emphasized, the possibility of there existing conditions of alienation in a transitionally socialist society such as their own, and they have discussed such special problems as those posed, for the construction of a post-capitalist society, by conflicts among small nationality groups, by the dominance of a charismatic leadership, and by competition among rival self-management organizations in different industries or even in the same industry.

Political authorities have found this sort of philosophizing disturbing, an encroachment upon their own domain. Ironically, in light of Marx's insistence on the need to unite practice with theory, some Yugoslav officials have complained of the *Praxis* philosophers' failure to limit their writings to purely theoretical, or 'scientific', subjects. Meanwhile, within Yugoslavia, the strains produced by fundamental disagreements over the advisability of reintroducing certain capitalist economic practices—notably market mechanisms—have become more evident during a time of international recession. These strains had already been brought to light at an earlier time by *Praxis* writers; these writers have now, at least, in some measure, shared the traditional fate of messengers of ill tidings. In order to remove the eight Belgrade philosophers from their teaching posts, the Serbian (regional) government was required, in effect, legislatively to abrogate the basic social principle of self-management as it applied to academic workers, since these individuals had repeatedly been upheld by votes of duly authorized groups of colleagues. This, I suspect, is a development of considerable historical significance. Perhaps the ultimate irony lies in the very traditional response made by officials of a supposedly 'new society', to critical analyses of that society by philosophers who have taken Marx's radicalism at face value.

In presenting this final variety of contemporary Marxism, I have placed greater stress on specific political and economic conditions than at any previous point in this book. This is as it should be, because the Yugoslav philosophers' most innovative contributions lie in the area of attempting to fill in, with reference to the actual, constantly changing state of affairs in their own country, Marx's open-ended 'vision of a possible future society of associated producers'. Although much could be said by way of more detailed criticism, both positive and negative, of the theoretical writings of various individual *Praxis* philosophers—for instance, concerning the excessive insistence of some of them on the term 'humanism' —I have refrained from such criticism in favour of pointing to the relevance of their work for assessing the practical applicability, present and future, of the philosophy of Marx.

The precise ways in which it is relevant remain to be determined; the matter is both too current and too complex to be resolved here. The future fate of Yugoslav philosophers is a matter of specu- lation, as is the effect that present and future political events will have on their philosophical writings. In my own speculations about this, I am reasonably sure of only two points: first, that some of the *Praxis* philosophers will continue to produce important philosophi- cal work, and second, that both what they write and what happens to the peculiar new social structures to which they have devoted so much of their critical attention will have an importance dispropor- tionately greater than the size of their small country.

Conclusion

Marxism, in one form or another, is an inescapable intellectual force almost everywhere in the modern world. In countries where books by, and sometimes even about, Marx are prohibited, often with severe sanctions attached, Marxism is at least as much in the air as in those lands where such books are standard items for the reading public. In the former countries, Marxism's presence is primarily that of a 'spectre', to use the apt expression of *The Communist Manifesto*.

Unfortunately, in some of the parts of the world in which works by and about Marx exist in the greatest profusion, the form that Marxism has taken is primarily that of an ideology. We considered, earlier in this book, the pejorative connotations that Marx himself attached to this term. But Louis Althusser, a particularly intelligent apologist for the strain of Marxism to which the label 'orthodox' has been attached, speaks for many proponents of Marxism as an ideology when he argues that ideology, though it is different from pure (social) 'science', will, so to speak, always be with us. This way of looking at the matter implies a justification for the reduction of Marxism to a set of catechism-like dogmas and ultimately to a set of empty slogans that has taken place so often over the past century, and that continues to take place today; all that is required is that the rare Marxist intellectual should grasp the 'scientific' truth with rigour and in depth.

My conviction is that Marxism is on the agenda at least in part because it ought to be—that is, because it provides a systematic conceptual framework both for understanding and for acting in the contemporary social world that is superior to all its rivals, and because large numbers of perceptive individuals have recognized this fact and responded to it; at the same time, the threat that one or more sloganized versions of it may be used by unscrupulous, opportunistic politicians to impose new structures of dominance and subordination on their societies remains formidable. In such circumstances, the only 'intellectual' whose existence remains viable is the pure ideologist, in Marx's original sense—that is, the pure, uncritical apologist for the existing order.

It has been a principal theme of this book that Marxism is, above all, a certain kind of critical thinking. Its dialectical methodology is, as Marx himself noted, a marvellous tool for engaging in the radical criticism of existing social structures and the thought-patterns that sustain them. What is best and most important about Marx's thought as description at various levels of generalization, including the description of capitalist economic structures to which he devoted greatest attention, is its capacity for developing conceptual categories that make plausible the existence of social states of affairs fundamentally different from the one being described. Marx's 'vision of a possible future', as I have shown, is, first and foremost, just his insistence on such a possibility, rather than being a detailed, positive blueprint.

The philosophy of Marx runs into the most trouble if it is construed either as somehow furnishing such a blueprint, particularly in the form of a prediction of just how history is bound to evolve, or as offering us a set of unquestionable metaphysical truths about the nature of the universe, in the grand style of classical or early modern philosophy. But, although Marx was no more perfectly clear, at every moment of his career, as to the precise purposes and parameters of his thought than any other significant thinker has ever been, the internal textual bases for supposing him to have construed it as blueprint or as metaphysics are flimsy at best, and the logical grounds for our so construing it are non-existent.

Marx's philosophy, then, is flexible and open. It lends itself to reinterpretation; indeed, given its sensitivity to historical change, it encourages reinterpretation. There exists no infallible set of criteria for deciding at just what point some alleged reformulation of, or creative addition to, Marxism has become non-Marxist. But only dogmatists will regard this as a serious problem.

At the same time, this flexibility and openness must not be identified with unboundedness or contentlessness. If one follows Marx's critical analyses, then one's overall perception of past history and of the contemporary social world is certain to be different, in a number of specifiable ways, from that of, let us say, a traditionalist or a liberal. One will, for instance, see something more significant in the history of the past three decades in Indo-China than a mere series of errors in policy judgement on the part of Western powers, and one will view the inflationary and recessionary difficulties of recent years in capitalist countries as something other than a mystery that an improved econometrics might enable us to fathom and solve.

Marx's own global thought-framework relies heavily, in its details, on a knowledge of economics, political science, history, and a number of other disciplines that are often treated in isolation from one another in our culture. It was the *philosophical* perspective which Marx brought to his apparently disparate studies that enabled him to sustain his sense of the interrelatedness of things, and thereby to exert the enormous historical influence that he still continues, nearly a century after his death, to do. The principal aim of this book has been to delineate that perspective and to point out some of its weaknesses and strengths.

Select Bibliography

Marx and Engels

Selected Works, Lawrence & Wishart, London, 1968; International Publishers, New York, 1968.
Contains, *inter alia*, their *Manifesto of the Communist Party*, Marx's Preface to *A Contribution to the Critique of Political Economy*, Marx's *Critique of the Gotha Programme* and *Theses on Feuerbach*, and Engels's *Socialism: Utopian and Scientific*, *The Origins of the Family, Private Property and the State*, and *Ludwig Feuerbach and the End of Classical German Philosophy*.
The German Ideology, Lawrence & Wishart, London, 1965; International Publishers, New York, 1965.

Marx

Capital, 3 vols., C. Dutt (ed.), Lawrence & Wishart, London, 1970–72; International Publishers, New York, 1967.
Early Texts, D. McLellan (tr. and ed.), Basil Blackwell, Oxford, 1971; Barnes & Noble, New York, 1971.
The Grundrisse: Foundations of the Critique of Political Economy, M. Nicolaus (tr.), Allen Lane and Penguin Books, London, 1973; Random House, New York, 1974.
Writings of the Young Marx on Philosophy and Society, Loyd D. Easton and Kurt H. Guddat (eds.), Doubleday & Co., Garden City, New York, 1967.
Contains, *inter alia*, *The German Ideology*, Part I, and *Theses on Feuerbach*.

Engels

The Condition of the Working Class in England, W. O. Henderson and W. H. Chaloner (tr.), Basil Blackwell, Oxford, 1971; Stanford University Press, Stanford, Calif., 1958.

Hegel

The Logic of Hegel, W. Wallace (tr.), 3rd ed., Oxford University Press, London and New York, 1975.
Philosophy of History, J. Sibree (tr.), Dover, New York, 1956.
Phenomenology of Mind, J. B. Baillie (tr.), Allen & Unwin, London, 1931; Humanities Press, New York, 1964.
Philosophy of Right, T. M. Knox (tr.), Oxford University Press, London and New York, 1942.
Science of Logic, Arnold Miller (tr.), Allen & Unwin, London, 1969; Humanities Press, New York, 1969.

Luxemburg

The Accumulation of Capital, A. Schwarzchild (tr.), Routledge & Kegan Paul, London, 1951; Monthly Review Press, New York, 1964.

Korsch

Marxism and Philosophy, Fred Halliday (tr.), New Left Books, London, 1970; Monthly Review Press, New York, 1971.

Gramsci

Prison Notebooks: Selections, Quintin Hoare and Geoffrey N. Smith (tr.), Lawrence & Wishart, London, 1971; International Publishers, New York, 1971.

Lenin

Selected Works, 3 vols., Lawrence & Wishart, London, 1964; International Publishers, New York, 1967.
Contains, *inter alia*, *State and Revolution* and *What is to be Done?*
Materialism and Empirio-Criticism, Lawrence & Wishart, London, 1958; International Publishers, New York, 1970.

Lukács

History and Class-Consciousness, Rodney Livingstone (tr.), Merlin Press, London, 1971; M.I.T. Press, Cambridge, Mass., 1971.

Sartre

Search for a Method, Hazel E. Barnes (tr.), Random House, New York, 1968.

Althusser

For Marx, B. R. Brewster (tr.), Allen Lane, London, 1970; Random House, New York, 1970.
Lenin and Philosophy and Other Essays, B. R. Brewster (tr.), New Left Books, London, 1971; Monthly Review Press, New York, 1972.

Petrovič

Marx in the Mid-Twentieth Century, Doubleday & Co., Garden City, New York, 1967.

Stojanović

Between Ideals and Reality: A Critique of Socialism and its Future, Gerson S. Sher (tr.), Oxford University Press, New York, 1973.

Marković

From Affluence to Praxis: Philosophy and Social Criticism, University of Michigan Press, Ann Arbor, Mich, 1974.

Index

absolute spirit, 32–4
accumulation, 21, 28, 61, 95, 121
  primitive, 119–20
Adorno, T., 146
alienation, 43, 85–9, 136
  in Hegel, 33–4
  in later thinkers, 151–2, 156–7,
    161–2
Althusser, L., 145, 158–60, 164
analytic philosophy, 21, 86, 160
anarchism, 137, 139
antagonistic and non-antagonistic
    contradictions, *see*
    contradictions
appearances, 32, 68, 100
Aristotle, 23–9, 63, 68, 94, 102
art, 23, 143, 146
atheism, 39–40, 83–4
Aufhebung, 56
automation, *see* technology

Bakunin, M., 139
base and superstructure, 73–4, 144
Bauer, B., 38
Benjamin, W., 146
Berkeley, G., 22
Bernstein, E., 122, 135, 142
Bloch, E., 145
bourgeoisie, 35, *see also* capitalist
    class
bureaucracy, 18, 157

capital, 95
  variable and constant, 120, 123
Capital, 27, 61
  commodity fetishism in, 110–11
  method of, 51–3
  object of, 103–4

references to future in, 129–30,
    133–4, 140
writing and editing of, 13–14, 44
capitalist class, 18, 61, 76–7, 98,
    117–21 *passim*
capitalist system:
  alienation in, 89
  in Hegel, 36
  in the political economists, 16,
    25
  Marx's account of, 61, 64, 93–7
  nature of class-struggle in,
    97–102
  objection to Marx's account of,
    102–10
  possible transition from, 120–1
Castro, F., 7
causality, 37, 58–60, 78–82 *passim*,
    157
centralization of the means of
    production, 95–7, 117, 121
civil society, 18, 35
Civil War in France, The, 13
class, concept of, 17–18, 98–102
class-conflict, *see* class-struggle
class-interests, 74
class-struggle, 18, 92–3
  in Lenin, 81, 127–8
  polarization of, 97–102
classless society, 18, 137
coercion, 149–50
cognition, reflection theory of,
    81–2, 149
commodities, 27, 94, 102, 104–5
  fetishism of, 27, 111–12
Communist League, 12
Communist Manifesto, The, 48,
    91–3, 139

class-struggle in, 98–9, 102
  writing of, 12
communist society, 66, 128–30,
  133–40 *passim*
Comte, A., 75, 159
*Condition of the Working Class in
  England in 1844, The,* 44
contradictions, 32, 56, 68, 93, 159
  antagonistic and non-antagonistic, 66
*Contribution to the Critique of
  Political Economy, A,* 15
criticism (critique), concept of, 16,
  68, 73, 132, 135–6
  as basis of Marx's economics,
  103–5
Critique of Dialectical Reason,
  154–8
Critique of the Gotha Programme,
  13, 125, 129, 139
Critique of Pure Reason, 16

Darwinism, 46
de Beauvoir, S., 145
demands, 107, *see also* supply and
  demand
Democritus, 22
Descartes, R., 155, 157
Destruction of Reason, The, 151
determinism, 15, 22, 45–6 124–5,
  142
dialectics, 49, 67–9
  as a common thought-pattern,
  54–7
  as law and as reality, 58–62
  as structural and as genetic,
  62–7
  Bernstein's rejection of, 142
  generality of, 57–8
  in Engels, 46
  in Hegel, 31, 50–8 *passim,* 62
  in Marx, 51–3, 58–69 *passim*
dialectics of nature, 47, 60, 90
Dialectics of Nature, 47, 90, 125
Dialectics of the Concrete, 147
dictatorship of the proletariat,
  see proletariat
dominance and subordination,

see master and servant (or
  slave)
dualism, 60, 82, 87, 157

economic factors, dominance of,
  15, 19, 110–14, 159
Ego and His Own, The, 38
1844 Manuscripts, 25, 30–1, 41,
  83–5 *passim,* 128–9
  as influence on later thinkers,
  144
end of philosophy, 74–5
Engels, F., 21 41, 42, 85
  co-author of the *Manifesto,* 78,
  93
  editor of *Capital,* Vols. II and
  III, 13–14, 88, 130
  influence on Marx, 43–8
  intellectual heir of Marx, 141–2
  on materialism, 80
  on nature and laws of nature,
  60, 90, 124–5
  on relativism, 75–6
  on the role of ideas, 73–4
  on the varieties of socialism,
  127–8
  popularizer of Marx, 17
Epicurus, 22
epiphenomenalism, 73–4
epistemological break, 158
essence(s), 32, 68, 100
  human, 26, 84–91, 129, 133–4,
  155
  in Feuerbach, 42–3
Essence of Christianity, The, 39–41
essentialism, 8, 75
ethics, *see* morality
exchange-values, 26–7, 94, 106–9
existentialism, 154–5
explanation, 19, 55, 100–1, 110
exploitation, rate of, *see* surplus-
  value, rate of

fetishism of commodities, *see*
  commodities, fetishism of
feudal society, 61, 63–4, 93, 111–14
Feuerbach, L., 39–43, 84–5
Flaubert, G., 154
Fourier, C., 127

Frankfurt School, 146
freedom, 22, 76–7 125, 129–33
    passim, 140
    in Engels, 45–6
    in Hegel, 36–7

Garaudy, R., 145
genetic approach, *see* structural
    approach
German-French Annals, The, 38, 42
German Ideology, The, 15 38, 42,
    71–3, 83
    description of communist
    society in, 129, 136
God, 40, 83, 85
    in Hegel, 33, 57, 50
Gramsci, A., 143
Greek philosophers, 22–9
Grundrisse, 55, 109

Habermas, J., 146
Hegel, G. W. F., 16, 18, 23, 25,
    29–38
    influence on later thinkers, 145,
    151
    on dialectics, 50–8 *passim,* 62
    on metaphysics, 21
Heidegger, M., 145, 160
Heller, A., 147
Henry VIII, 112
Heraclitus, 21
Herr Vogt, 13
Hess, M., 38
historicism, 78
history, 48, 65–6, 77–8, 92–3,
    114–15
    class-struggle in, 97–102
    in Sartre, 156
    role of economic factors in,
    110–14, *see also Philosophy
    of History, The*
History and Class Consciousness,
    143, 150–3
Hobbes, T., 24
Holy Family, The, 13, 38
Housing Question, The, 75
humanism, 25, 85–6, 158–9, 162
Hume, D., 7, 22, 130
Husserl, E., 7, 154

idealism, 11, 72, 82, 87
    Feuerbach's rejection of, 40–1
    in Hegel, 25, 34–5, 58
ideology, 24, 42, 71–5, 131–3, 165
    in Althusser, 158
immediacy, 32, 54
immiseration, *see* improverishment
imperialism, 35, 96, 122, 142
impoverishment, 122
individuals, 61–2, 142, 155
inevitability, 14, 117–26 *passim*
intellectual activity, 87–8, 136–7
intellectuals, 99, 164–5
International Working-men's
    Association, 13
Internationale, The, 18
iron law of wages, 125

Jewish Question, On the, 38
joint-stock companies, 121
justice, 75–6, 131–3, 137

Kant, I., 7, 16, 53, 68, 151
Kautsky, K., 142
Khrushchev, N., 146
Kolakowski, L., 146–7
Korsch, K., 143
Košik, K., 147

labour, 33–4, 63, 87–9, 94–5,
    102–10 *passim*
labour power, *see* labour
labour theory of value, *see* labour
landlords (landowners), 61, 98
law (legal system), 137–8, 143
Law of the Tendency of the Rate
    of Profit to Fall, 122–3
law(s):
    in Engels, 45–7, 90
    in Hegel, 50
    of nature, 24–5, 29
    of society, 51–2, 59–60, 123–5
Lefebvre, H., 145
Leibniz, G. W., 22
Lenin, V. I., 7, 17, 30, 118, 147–50
    on materialism, 79–83
    relationships to other thinkers,
    152, 158
Lévi-Strauss, C., 158

174   *The Philosophy of Marx*

Life of Jesus, 39
Locke, J., 21, 22, 24
Logic (of Hegel), 30–2, 50
*Ludwig Feuerbach and the End of
   Classical German Philosophy,*
   39, 85
Lukács, G., 143, 150–3
Lumpenproletariat, 98
Luther, M., 28
Luxemburg, R., 142–3

*Manifesto of the Communist Party,
   see Communist Manifesto, The*
Mao Tse-tung, 7, 66–7, 144
Marcuse, H., 146
Marković, M., 160
Marr, N. Y., 144
Marxism and Philosophy, 143
master and servant (or slave),
   33–4, 57, 88–9, 102
   in Aristotle, 24
materialism, 21 40–3 *passim,*
   79–84
*Materialism and Empirio-
   Criticism,* 79–82
mechanism, 22, 80, 87
mediation, 56
Merleau-Ponty, M., 145
metaphysical mode of thinking,
   21, 46
method of inquiry and method of
   presentation, 52, 60
'Method of Political Economy,
   The', 63
morality, 61, 73, 78–9, 131–3, 137–8
   in later Marxists, 146, 150
Morgan, L., 78
Münzer, T., 145
Mussolini, B., 143

natural law, *see* law(s) of nature
naturalism, 22, 25
nature, 24–6, 129
   human, *see* essence(s), human
needs, 19, 26–7, 107–8, 136
   system of, 35
negation, 54–6, 62–3, 136
negation of the negation, *see*
   negation

objectification, 152
operationalism, 102, 106–10 *passim*
organic composition of capital, 95
orthodoxy, 8, 143, 155–6, 161, 164
over-determination, 159
Owen, R., 127

Paris Commune, 101–2
particularity, 35, 55, 61
party, vanguard, 17, 148–9, 151–2,
   153
Pashukanis, E. B., 143
petite bourgeoisie, 98, 101, 155
Petrović, G., 160
phenomenological method(s),
   32–3, 60, 154
Phenomenology of Spirit, The, 32–4
Philosophical Notebooks, 81
Philosophy of History, The, 36–7,
   57, 114–15, 130
Philosophy of Right, The. 34–6
Plato, 23, 75
Plekhanov, G., 142
political economy, 15–16, 25, 35,
   60–1, 103–4
Politics, 24, 26–8, 102
Popper, K., 78
positivism, 46, 74–5, 159
praxis, 22, 42, 86–9, 156–7
Praxis, 160–3
price, 102–6
primitive accumulation, *see*
   accumulation
Principle of Hope, The, 145
private property, 18, 61, 121, 136
   expropriation of, 97, 117, 139
profit, 94, 104
   rate of fall of, 122–4
proletariat, 17–19, 76–7, 98–9,
   117–19
   dictatorship of the, 149
   in Lukács, 151
property, *see* private property
psychic phenomena, 84

realm of freedom, *see* freedom
reason (in Hegel), 35
reductionism, 114
reification, 150–1

relativism, 45, 75–6
religion, 39–43, 83, 85, 111–14
revolution, 61, 96–7, 116, 120,
    135
  in Aristotle, 102
  in Lenin, 148–9
  in Sartre, 156–7
Reysner, M. A., 143
Ruge, A., 38

Saint-Simon, Comte de, 127
Sartre, J.-P., 154–8
scarcity, 29, 156–7
Schaff, A., 146, 157
science, 25, 45–7, 90, 124–5, 128
  in Althusser, 158–9, 164
Search for a Method, 154–6
slavery, 23–4, 37, *see also* master
    and servant (or slave)
Smith, A., 16, 84, 88, 103–4
Social Democratic Party, 13, 142,
    148
socialism, 16, 21, 127–8, 131, 135
Socialism: Utopian and Scientific,
    127–8
socialist realism, 153
socialization of labour, 97, 117,
    121
society of associated producers, 16,
    65–6, 117, 129, 135
species-being, 41, 43, 84
spheres of production and
    circulation, 53, 68–9, 100
Spirit of Utopia, 145
spontaneity, 148
Stalin, J., 144, 157
Stalinism, 161
State, 18, 34–6, 137
State and Revolution, 82, 149
Stirner, M., 38
Stojanović, S., 160
Strauss, D., 39
structural approach (contrasted
    with genetic approach), 64–7,
    95, 113, 158
supply and demand, 104–5, *see
    also* demands

surplus-value, 21, 28, 95, 127
  rate of, 123–4

technology, 26, 95–6, 109, 129
  in Aristotle, 24
  in Habermas, 146
Theories of Surplus-Value, 52
theory and practice, unity of, 19,
    144
Theses on Feuerbach, 8, 26, 39–40,
    84–90 *passim*
time (temporality), 77
Tito (J. Broz), 161
totality, 8, 56, 153
trade union consciousness, 118–19
trade unions, 94
transcendental entities, 60, 67, 77,
    80
transformative method, 40–1
triadicity, 53–6
Tribune, New York, 13

understanding (in Hegel), 35, 50
unemployed, industrial reserve
    army of the, 96
universal class, 18, 31, 99
universality, 55, 61
upheaval, anticipated Europe-wide,
    14, *see also* revolution
use-value, 26–7, 107
usury, 28

value, concept of, 102–10 *passim*,
    see also labour
values, 130–2
Vyshinsky, A., 143

wages, 94–6, 104, 120, 123
wealth, 95, 103–4
Wealth of Nations, The, 103
Weber, M., 130, 151
What Is To Be Done?, 149
will, 51, 62
Wittgenstein, L., 7

Young Hegelians, 30, 38–40, 44
Yugoslav Marxism, 160–3